# Workplace Skills in Practice

## Case Studies of Technical Work

Cathleen Stasz
Kimberly Ramsey
Rick Eden
Elan Melamid
Tessa Kaganoff

RAND, Santa Monica, CA

National Center for Research in Vocational Education
University of California, Berkeley
2150 Shattuck Avenue, Suite 1250
Berkeley, CA 94720-1674

Supported by
The Office of Vocational and Adult Education,
U.S. Department of Education

## FUNDING INFORMATION

Project Title              National Center for Research in Vocational Education

Grant Number               V051A30003-95A/V051A30004-95A

Act Under Which            Carl D. Perkins Vocational Education Act
Funds Administered:        P.L .98-524

Source of Grant:           Office of Vocational and Adult Education
                           U.S. Department of Education
                           Washington, D.C. 20202

Grantee:                   The Regents of the University of California
                           c/o National Center for Research in Vocational Education
                           2150 Shattuck Ave., Suite 1250
                           Berkeley, CA 94720-1674

Director:                  David Stern

Percent of Total
Grant Financed by
Federal Money:             100%

Dollar Amount
of Federal Funds
for Grant:                 $6,000,000

Disclaimer:                This publication was prepared pursuant to a grant with the Office of Vocational and Adult Education, U.S. Department of Education. Grantees undertaking such projects under government sponsorship are encouraged to express freely their judgment in professional and technical matters. Point of view or opinions do not, therefore, necessarily represent official U.S. Department of Education position or policy.

Discrimination:            Title VI of the Civil Rights Act of 1964 states: "No person in the United States shall, on the ground of race, color, or national origin, be excluded from participation in, be denied the benefits of, or be subjected to discrimination under any program or activity receiving federal financial assistance." Title IX of the Education Amendments of 1972 states: "No person in the United States shall, on the basis of sex, be excluded from participation in, be denied the benefits of, or be subjected to discrimination under any education program or activity receiving federal financial assistance." Therefore, the National Center for Research in Vocational Education projects, like every program or activity receiving financial assistance from the U.S. Department of Education, must be operated in compliance with these laws.

## PREFACE

This study explores skills and work-related dispositions in technical work. It adopts a sociocultural approach to closely examine skills in seven target jobs in worksites representing diverse industries—health care, traffic management, transportation, and semiconductor manufacturing. It explores employers' strategies for obtaining the skills they need under conditions of technological or organizational change.

The report should interest employers, industry groups, and policy-makers at all levels of government who are concerned with changes in the modern workplace and the impact of those changes on work-force skills. It should also be of interest to school administrators and teachers who are implementing school reforms that attempt to im-prove youth transition from school to work.

This research was supported by the National Center for Research in Vocational Education, University of California, Berkeley. The Center, funded by the Office of Adult and Vocational Education, U.S. Department of Education, engages in research and development ac-tivities designed to increase the access of all Americans to a high-quality work life. The study was conducted in RAND's Institute on Education and Training (IET).

# CONTENTS

# TABLES

## SKILL REQUIREMENTS IN THE NEW WORKPLACE

Many believe that the workplace has changed dramatically in response to a new competitive business environment that is marked by flexibility, fast response time, and managerial and technological innovations. This new workplace is thought to require workers with higher and more varied skills, particularly general skills such as problem solving; unfortunately, schools are not perceived to be producing students who have such skills. The result, it is commonly argued, is a "skills gap" that threatens American productivity and competitiveness.

## RESEARCH OBJECTIVES AND APPROACH

The goal of the research reported here was to improve the understanding of skills as they are manifested in technical work, both by extending the theoretical conception of skills and by providing empirical observations of skills in practice. We also wanted to better understand the institutional context in which working activities—particularly learning on-the-job—take place because we view skills as a feature of the workplace as a social system, and not just features of individuals or jobs.

Our study sample included sites in four firms that represent diverse business areas: a transportation agency (TA), a traffic management agency (TM), a microprocessor manufacturer (MPM), and a health care agency (HA). The number of personnel in these firms range from 26 people to tens of thousands. Two firms, TM and TA, are public agencies; the other two are private. Three have service functions, while one (MPM) is a product manufacturer. They serve markets of varying scale, from local (TM), to regional (TA), national (HA), and international (MPM). Most of these sites were feeling the pinch of austerity. Almost all the workers we observed were facing rapid changes in technology and in the way their work was done. In addition, three firms had begun using new management practices such as total quality management (TQM), continuous quality improvement (CQI), or organizational learning to guide restructuring of many aspects of their operations.

At these four worksites we studied skills in practice in seven service and manufacturing jobs:

- Traffic signal technicians working in the traffic management agency,

- Home health aides and licensed vocational nurses (LVNs) in the health care agency,

- Test cell associates and equipment technicians in the microprocessor manufacturing firm, and

- Construction inspectors and survey inspectors at the transportation agency.

Over several days we observed workers' everyday activities and interviewed the workers about their backgrounds (e.g., previous education and training experiences) and current job and work experiences. We also interviewed senior managers, staff, line managers, and human resource personnel to obtain information regarding each firm and its policies.

We focused on three skill areas—problem solving, communications, and teamwork—as well as work-related dispositions; all have generally been perceived to be required in the workforce. For instance, the new workplace emphasizes a shift in decisionmaking and problem solving from the supervisory level to the shop floor, where workers must cope on the spot with a growing number of unpredictable problems. Communications skills, both with speech and text, are widely cited as among the most important skills needed by today's workers. Many discussions of new skill requirements in the workforce mention teamwork as a necessary skill.  Much attention has been paid to the dispositions needed to succeed on the job; indeed, some studies suggest that the skills "gap" identified by employers may be more about dispositions than academic or technical skills.

Specifically, we set out to determine the following:

- Are generic skills and work-related dispositions evident in performing the job?  How do workers conceive of them?  How do skills and dispositions vary across jobs and work contexts?

- How do firms view skill requirements, and how do these views affect human resource policies such as recruitment, hiring, and training?

- What formal and informal relationships do firms have with education providers, including secondary and postsecondary training institutions, to acquire and develop skilled workers?

## FINDINGS AND CONCLUSIONS

This study demonstrates that work context matters in the consideration of skills.  Workplaces are complex, dynamic social systems that defy simplistic categorization of skills and straightforward matching of skill requirements to jobs.  The study provides a rich picture of skills and dispositions in work and draws the following conclusions:

- Generic skills and dispositions are important in work and to workers.

- Generic skills and dispositions vary with work context.

- Employers do not necessarily understand the skill requirements of their frontline workforce.

- Employers may lack effective strategies for acquiring workforce skills.

- Employers do little to foster skill development among nonmanagerial workers and sometimes take courses of action that undermine skill development.

- Employers have weak connections with education providers for supporting acquisition or development of workforce skills.

## SKILLS AND DISPOSITIONS IN PRACTICE

We observed generic skills and work-related dispositions to be important in work and found this importance to be salient to the workers.  Our interviews and work observations enabled us to see how workers actually apply skills in the context of their jobs, communities of practice, and work settings.  However, we found that required skills can vary substantially by these contexts.  Employers did not always appear to understand just how skills are realized on the job.

### Problem Solving

We were able to analyze how workers solve both routine and atypical problems and how problem solving is construed by their community of practice.  For example, construction inspectors understand problem solving in their work in the context of quality assurance and control.  A typical inspection problem occurs when an inspector identifies a discrepancy between the specifications and the construction and then must identify the source of the discrepancy and how to get the error corrected.  Survey inspectors view problem solving similarly; however, unlike any of the other jobs we studied, survey inspection requires mathematical problem solving.  By contrast, problem solving for the home health care worker and the LVN is primarily situation assessment.  The worker is the "eyes and ears" of an extended patient care team, where each patient represents a "problem" that needs resolution.  For the equipment technicians at MPM and traffic signal technicians who maintain and repair electronic equipment, problem solving generally means troubleshooting.  When the equipment or system breaks down, they must know how to troubleshoot—to identify the problem and fix it.

### Communications

Required communications skills varied similarly.  An important distinction for frontline workers was internal versus external audiences—members of their own firms versus members of "the public," including their firm's customers. For example, communication with patients and their families was a central part of the job of home health providers. Traffic signal engineers working in the field often had to communicate with motorists, the "customers" of the traffic signal system. However, with the possible exception of home health aides, most workers communicated chiefly with internal audiences—members of their work group, co-workers, and supervisors. Finally, the workers in our study communicated with audiences who were single individuals or small groups.

In both speech and writing, the most common purpose for communications skills was to convey an appropriate fact accurately. Home health providers reported on the status of patient functioning and logged their own activities, including facts such as mileage driven. Survey inspectors called out measurements. The second most common purpose was to convey procedural information—instructions. Accuracy, speed, and clarity are highly valued. An amicable and professional demeanor was highly valued in all spoken communications. Such a demeanor was perceived to improve the ability and willingness of the listener to engage in communication. This was particularly important on jobs that required the worker to communicate directly with the public.

## Teamwork

Teamwork is a description of how work is organized. What constitutes a "team" is subject to local definition and thus must be defined in relation to the working context. Thus, the "skill" or "interpersonal competency" needed to participate in a team will depend on the work organization. For instance, a self-managing work group is an intact and definable social system, with a defined piece of work and authority to manage the task on its own. This traditional conception of self-managing work groups generally characterizes teamwork in two jobs: survey inspectors and test cell associates. A second important characteristic of the work teams is the distribution of knowledge, skills, and sometimes authority among individuals. Teams can be formally recognized and supported by the organization, or informally constituted by team members themselves. The survey inspector team, for example, is comprised of individuals of different rank and skill, with party chief as the acknowledged leader. Home health providers are members of a large managed-care team, characterized by both distributed knowledge and authority linked to special certification. Construction inspectors operate as members of a "virtual" team, which helps improve the quality and efficiency of their work. Traffic signal technicians and test technicians (MPM) work independently for the most part, but they may form field teams for short-term problem solving or specific activities.

## Work-Related Dispositions

Dispositions or "habits of mind"—individuals' tendencies to put their capabilities into action—are thought to influence how individuals deal with various situations. Since the concept of dispositions appears to subsume both motivation and volition, we use this term in our analysis. Some respondents discussed feelings and interpersonal relationships, such as a sense of closeness or mutual respect, as being important qualities. We incorporate these characteristics into our analysis as well. The survey inspectors possess three important dispositions for work. Because their jobs require teamwork, the survey inspectors emphasize cooperation. They also stress a disposition for attending to details and exactness. This emphasis on quality derives from their professional standards as surveyors. Construction inspectors also must have a conscientious attitude toward their work. Because home health providers spend most of their time visiting patients at home, they must be independent in their work habits. They must also be flexible and tolerant of oversight. Home care workers must be patient, friendly, and sensitive to a range of cultures and socioeconomic conditions. Technicians at MPM need to be flexible and adaptable to change, since the technology evolves quickly even though the tasks are repetitive. For test cell technicians, the most important attitudes are the ability to work as part of the team, to be flexible to the work assignments—working on different machines, on different shifts, and sometimes on Saturdays—and to be "eager and willing to learn." Technicians need to work independently with little supervision and to accommodate the variability of the job—a normal slow pace punctuated by emergency calls. They also need to be motivated to keep up with technology changes on their own.

## ACQUIRING AND DEVELOPING WORKFORCE SKILLS

Firms have several options for responding to new skill demands created by technological, management, or work process innovations and to regulatory changes: hire employees with certain skills, produce skills in their own training program, contract with outside agencies or individuals to provide training, or create incentives that encourage workers to invest in their own skills. Generally, we found that firms lacked effective strategies for acquiring needed skills in their workforce. They did little to foster skill development among nonmanagerial workers and sometimes had policies that undermined skill development.

### Hiring and Training

At TA, a merger and adoption of TQM in one division have hampered hiring and training in the agency itself. Instead, individual firms and their subcontractors have responsibility for training construction inspectors. Contractors formed a consortium for planning, training, and trainer hiring. For survey inspectors, training is integrated with their standards of professional practice and includes a combination of union-provided training, on-the-job training (OJT) in line with professional standards, and limited formal classes to meet mandatory requirements, such as safety-related training.

TM, finding that experienced traffic signal technicians are at a premium, has adopted a "grow your own" strategy and identifies appropriate "growable" candidates with coursework or degrees in electronics or digital systems. However, it has no budget for training programs, despite significant changes in technology and agency liability for maintenance. It relies on OJT as a skill development strategy.

MPM hires skilled workers and has a training program that is connected to the firm's strategic plan and reflects its recent adoption of total quality management (TQM) principles. The firm makes use of OJT, dedicated trainers, and outside consultants to provide general training. HA provides continuous training opportunities, both elective and mandatory, for all levels of the workforce to meet both individual job and institutional certification. Training is tied to career development programs for nurses, aides, and other staff.

## Connections to Schools

As a group, the firms we studied did not have strong connections with education providers for supporting acquisition or development of workforce skills. The two smallest firms, TM and MPM, have no formal connections to schools. The two larger firms, TA and HA, have links with local high schools. HA has relationships with magnet schools and career academy programs in local high schools and encourages employees to use the tuition reimbursement program to upgrade skills.

Although our sample of jobs and worksites is small, the issues raised in this research are not unique to these cases. Our detailed observations provide interesting and instructive examples from which others can learn, and our conclusions should encourage reconsideration of basic assumptions about skill requirements and skill acquisition that underlie current approaches to reforming schools and to setting skill standards. The study also suggests fruitful lines of research that take a sociocultural approach to the twin problems of understanding and meeting skill requirements.

# ACKNOWLEDGMENTS

First and foremost, we thank the individuals who gave us access to their work and workplaces and who participated in the study. Although confidentiality agreements prevent thanking them by name, their cooperation and support made the study possible.

Though responsibility for the final product is ours alone, we benefitted from excellent reviews of an early draft by Steve Barley and Sally Ann Law that helped us refocus and clarify the study findings. We also thank Tom Bailey and John Wirt for their thoughtful suggestions.

Roger Benjamin, director of RAND's Institute on Education and Training, provided funding to complete the study analysis and publication.

The late Charles S. Benson, who directed NCRVE from 1988 to 1993, was generous in his praise and encouragement for this research and our earlier studies on generic skills. We dedicate this work to his mcmory.

# Chapter One

# INTRODUCTION

## THE NEW WORKPLACE

It has become commonplace to argue that the workplace has changed dramatically in response to a new competitive business environment that is marked by flexibility, fast response time, and managerial and technological innovations. Work organization is now, the argument goes, increasingly characterized by the integration of traditionally separate functional roles (e.g., design, engineering, manufacturing) and flatter organizational hierarchies with decentralization of responsibility and greater employee involvement. Innovation and speed are accomplished through teams of workers who monitor quality and take charge of reconfiguring the production process, thereby performing some of the supervisory, planning, repair, maintenance, and support functions previously the responsibility of managers or specialists. Compared to the traditional model of work, based largely on mass production, this new "flexible" model is thought to require less supervision but workers with higher and more varied skills.[1]

It is also commonly asserted that students are ill-prepared for the future workplace and that they need new kinds of skills to perform

---

[1]There is a large, growing literature on flexible production systems and new processes embedded in such systems, such as total quality management, just-in-time supply, quality circles, and the like (see Levine and Luck, 1994). In addition, comparative analyses examine broader institutional and cultural contexts to determine the economic and social forces that support the flexible model, including education and training systems (see Finegold, 1992; Finegold and Soskice, 1988; Soskice, 1991).

well. The dominant source of evidence that workers need new job skills comes from employer surveys and interviews. Natriello (1989) reviewed 14 studies of employer needs that focused on entry-level workers. He found that employers most often cited the importance of employee attitudes, followed by an emphasis on "generic" skills such as problem solving and communications over job-specific skills. And in a recent national survey, employers ranked applicants' attitude and communication skills as the most important factors in hiring decisions (National Center on the Educational Quality of the Workforce, 1995). The conclusion that employers seem relatively satisfied with workers' technical skills, but see a need for increasing generic skills and/or improving workers attitudes or dispositions, has been corroborated in a number of studies (e.g., Bikson and Law, 1994; Hudis et al., 1992; Cappelli, 1992).

One response to the perceived "skills gap"—the mismatch between the existing workforce skills supply and the skill demands in the new workplace—has been to redefine skill needs to reflect employer concerns. This redefinition shifts the focus from job-specific skills to general skills and adds other factors, such as attitudes or prosocial behaviors, that are not typically defined as "skills." While several conceptions of new skills have been put forward, two will serve as illustrative examples. One conception, offered in a recent book by Marshall and Tucker, sums up "the emerging consensus on the skills needed to power a modern economy" (1992, p. 80) as follows: a high capacity for abstract, conceptual thinking; the ability to apply that capacity effectively to complex, real-world problems that may change as jobs evolve; the ability to communicate effectively, particularly when communicating within work groups, on highly technical topics, and with computer-based media; and the ability to work well with others as well as independently, with relatively little supervision.

Another conception is presented in several influential reports issued by the former Secretary of Labor's Commission on Achieving Necessary Skills (SCANS, 1991, 1992a; 1992b). SCANS defines three "foundation skills" (basic skills, thinking skills, and personal qualities) and five work "competencies" that effective workers can productively use (resources, interpersonal skills, information, systems, and technology) (SCANS, 1991). In the SCANS framework, competencies and foundations are generic, in the sense that "most of them are required for most jobs" (SCANS, 1992b) and are distinct from technical knowledge (SCANS, 1991).

A second response to the perceived skills gap is seen in school reform proposals. These proposals redefine what skills students should learn and how they should be taught. [2] Reforms advocate significant changes to the curriculum such as integrating academic and vocational education, teaching "all aspects" of the industry, and teaching general skills (e.g., problem solving, communication) in addition to purely academic or vocational subjects. Following new models of learning advanced by research in cognitive science (e.g., Stasz et al., 1993; Collins, Brown, and Newman, 1989; Raizen, 1989), reformers also advocate different approaches to classroom instruction, including more student-centered instruction, small-group and cooperative instruction, and project-based learning. Some argue that school-based learning should be integrated with work-based experience because some skills can best be learned on the job (Bailey, 1993a; Kazis, 1993). The School-to-Work Opportunities Act of 1994 (STWOA) emphasizes the integration of school-based and work-based learning as a program requirement.

Proposals that redefine curriculum and instruction need to be sensitive to the fact that perceived skill requirements in a changing economy present several challenges for educators. First, the content of academic curricula is generally organized by subject area and vocational instruction is often job-specific.[3] Such organization focuses on instruction within a domain and emphasizes the development of knowledge and skills particular to that domain. Second, the reforms add work-related attitudes or dispositions to the list of competencies that students should acquire. Attitudes and dispositions are inevitably tied to beliefs and values, which schools often avoid teaching explicitly for a host of reasons. Third, most proposals fail to sufficiently specify how to turn recommendations for new curriculum

---

[2]For example, see the School-to-Work Opportunities Act of 1994; National Center for Research in Vocational Education, 1995; National Assessment of Vocational Education, 1994.

[3]Although the 1990 Amendments to the Perkins Act sought to broaden vocational education beyond job-specific training, the pace of changes is slow, and most school systems are trying to fit reforms into existing curricula rather than making broader curriculum changes (National Assessment of Vocational Education (NAVE), 1994).

content and pedagogical practices into instructional design strategies. This is particularly problematic for reforms that emphasize project-based or applied-learning approaches in which students learn and practice skills in "real-world" or "authentic" contexts. Teachers are typically trained and certified to teach along disciplinary lines. They have little opportunity to observe work contexts outside of school or otherwise gain the knowledge they need to contextualize teaching in ways that reformers envision (Stasz et al., 1993).[4]

The skill standards movement represents another response wherein reformers hope to effect changes in education that will extend to the workplace. According to its proponents, skill standards and certification should improve the fit between what is learned in school and what is needed on the job, thereby facilitating the school-to-work transition and strengthening the country's economic position (Commission on Skills of the American Workforce, 1990). Another rationale behind the skill standards movement is to create a better certification system for the participating industries. A certification system can indicate to students what they must learn, provide motivation for acquiring particular skills needed in the workforce, and provide better access to a national labor market (if certifications are portable and recognized nationally). At the national level, the skill standards movement is cemented by federally sponsored pilot projects to develop skill standards in 22 industries and by the recently appointed National Skills Standards Board, established in the *Goals 2000: Educate America Act* (Bailey and Merritt, unpublished). These arguments for establishing a skill standards system are logical, although there are no studies on whether standards and certification will have the desired effects.

---

[4]The authors of the SCANS report, whose recommendations have been adopted by program designers and school-change advocates, caution that "the SCANS workplace competencies will not be widely taught unless teachers have access to instructional materials that *put them in context*" (SCANS, *Learning a Living: A Blueprint for High Performance*, 1992a, p. 45; italics added).

## THE DEBATE OVER WORKPLACE SKILLS

As we have indicated, the current debate over the perceived "skills gap" lacks a clear and common conceptual framework (Berryman and Bailey, 1992). This creates several problems for defining skill needs and for devising education, training, or other policies to adequately respond to the concerns at hand. A basic problem centers on the concept of skill requirements and related definitions of work and skills. The concept of skill requirements is generally used to analyze both the characteristics of jobs (e.g., tasks, roles) and of the individuals who perform them (e.g., aptitudes, abilities, characteristics) (Attewell, 1990; Darrah, 1994; Spenner, 1990). Jobs are analyzed to establish what individuals will need to know and do in order to perform them.[5] These job requirements, in turn, become prescriptions for education or training designed to prepare individuals for the job. Filling the "skills gap" is an exercise in matching people to jobs. Reforms to education or skill standardization and certification, mentioned above, are meant to assist in this process.

This concept of skill requirements, however, largely ignores the work context by viewing the workplace as a backdrop to individual actions. Absent is the idea—borne out in many studies of actual work—that workplaces are shaped by human choice and by the actions taken by those who work in them (Darrah, 1992, 1994; Scribner and Sachs, 1990; Billett, 1993; Lave and Wenger, 1991; Orr, 1991; Barley, 1995). Characteristics of the workplace can also structure action—work processes, technology in use, and incentives and disincentives for workers to learn and use skills. Learning work is not just a process of internalizing knowledge and skills "required" on the job, but a social activity.

An analysis of skill requirements that ignores work context draws attention away from workplace characteristics and possible shortcomings in firm behavior that affect skill utilization and performance, including poor management, fear of empowering workers, pursuit of low-wage options such as offshore production, and the depression of

---

[5]Traditional methods for defining job and task requirements produce narrowly defined task lists that ignore organizational and work context factors. While these methods are still in use, they may be inadequate for assessing skill needs in the flexible workplace (Bailey and Merritt, unpublished; Hanser, 1995).

wages, benefits, and working conditions (Ray and Mickelson, 1993; Teixeira and Mishel, 1993).  Despite employers' concern that front-line workers will need new skills to be productive in the workplace, research consistently shows that they invest less in skills of production-level workers than in employees with higher educational background:  the bulk of firm-based training goes to managerial, sales, and professional workers (Lillard and Tan, 1986; Vaughn and Berryman, 1989).  When employers do provide training to production-level workers, they tend to invest sporadically in "customized" training geared toward specific skills (e.g., when new technology is implemented), rather than in broad training in generic skills (Rogers and Streeck, 1991).  Furthermore, typical workplace training programs have been designed with the traditional model of work organization in mind, and are likely inappropriate for teaching the kinds of worker knowledge, skills, and attitudes desired under the flexible model emerging now (Bailey, 1993a).[6]  A review of worker training conducted by Congress' Office of Technology Assessment (OTA, 1990) concluded that classroom instruction is still the most common formal training method in the United States.  Finally, studies emphasize formal training and its associated costs and benefits.  They do not explore how individuals learn on the job through self-study, informal instruction by a co-worker, or the social organization that supports learning in the workplace.

In sum, an analysis of the skills gap that ignores the workplace itself has helped shape a somewhat one-sided public discourse that blames the gap on individuals who lack skills and on educational institutions that fail to adequately teach them.  It focuses policy on reforming schools or creating standards for individuals to achieve and pays less attention to workplace reforms that might improve skills and productivity.

## RESEARCH OBJECTIVES AND APPROACH

The goal of the research reported here was to expand our understanding of skills and work-related dispositions as they are consti-

---

[6]A similar conclusion has been reached with respect to publicly funded literacy or remedial skills programs linked to vocational education and job training programs (Grubb, Kalman, et al., 1991; Schultz, 1992).

tuted in technical work. Following sociocultural perspectives (e.g., Vygotsky, 1978), we view skills as a feature of the workplace as a social system, and not just features of individuals or jobs. Specifically, we went beyond the general skills or competencies, as described by SCANS and others, to illuminate the variations and similarities in "generic" competencies that occur in work practice. This shift is important for several reasons discussed earlier: most recent research suggests that general skills must configure to the work context, and an appreciation of this context can help educators and employers clarify what should be taught and develop more effective educational and training activities.

Second, we wanted to develop our understanding of the influence of dispositions on work behavior. Research has typically separated cognition from affective behaviors, while recognizing that both play a role in competent performance. Our previous studies of teaching generic skills for the workplace show that effective teachers emphasize noncognitive behaviors, like taking responsibility for one's actions or applying effort to a task. Similarly, many employers appear to value attitude over experience or technical skill in their hiring decisions, and voice concerns that new applicants lack an appropriate "work ethic". Schools fall short in developing appropriate dispositions toward work.

Third, we wanted to expand our understanding of the institutional context in which working activities—particularly learning on-the-job—take place. Just as school can affect teaching and learning activities through policies related to teacher professionalism or press for achievement (e.g., Stasz et al., 1990, 1993), human resource policies in firms can determine how work is organized, who gets trained, or how performance is rewarded. By examining aspects of the social organization of work at the level of the firm or enterprise, we can observe the relationship between work activities in a particular community of practice and the larger organization that helps shape work practice.

Our research approach employed multiple methods to examine skills and work-related attitudes in seven service and manufacturing jobs in the subbaccalaureate labor market. These jobs were selected from local sites in Los Angeles that were experiencing changes that affected skill demands of their technical workers, such as technology implementation or workplace restructuring.  Specifically, we set out to determine the following:

- What generic skills and work-related dispositions are evident in performing these jobs?  How do workers conceive of them?  How do the skills and dispositions vary across jobs and work contexts?

- How do firms view skill requirements, and how do these views affect human resource policies such as recruitment, hiring, and training?

- What formal and informal relationships do firms have with education providers, including secondary and postsecondary training institutions, to acquire and develop skilled workers?

## ORGANIZATION OF THIS REPORT

Following this Introduction, the report is divided into five chapters. Chapter Two discusses the study's conceptual approach and research methods.  Chapter Three describes the firms and jobs we studied.  Chapter Four characterizes the skills and work-related dispositions in those jobs.  Chapter Five describes firms' responses to skill needs.  The final chapter presents our conclusions and discusses implications of the study for the current debate about skills, for school and skill standards reforms, and for future research.

# Chapter Two

# RESEARCH APPROACH AND METHODS

## WORK IN CONTEXT

As discussed in Chapter One, our approach to studying skills at work assumes that skill needs must be examined in the context of work from the perspective of individuals engaged in that working community. The conceptual underpinnings of this approach stem from sociocultural theories, which argue that the social setting in which cognitive activity takes place is an integral part of that activity, not just the surrounding context for it (Lave 1988, 1991; Resnick, 1991; Rogoff and Charajay, 1995; Scribner, 1984, 1988; Vygotsky, 1978). The knowledge, attitudes, and abilities needed for a particular job can be understood only within a particular working context, from the perspective of individuals in the social setting. The context of the social setting can include other actors, the task at hand, the organization of the work, the physical or symbolic systems that comprise the job, and so on (Hart-Landsberg et al., 1992; Martin and Beach, 1992; Resnick, 1991; Scribner, 1984, 1988).

Within a social setting, work is often situated in communities of practice that share preferred ways of doing a task, establish standards for performance, and shape a newcomer's introduction to the working group (Lave and Wenger, 1991). The kind of information that a community of practice shares may lie outside the scope of officially designed jobs and include information about the group itself, such as informal status hierarchies and hidden communication networks (Levine and Moreland, 1991). Individuals and communities reside in workplaces defined by technology, organization, and activities that can constrain or support use and development of skills (Darrah, 1992).

This conceptual approach suggests a multilevel analysis of skills that takes at least three perspectives into account—individuals performing the work, the communities of practice, and the broader organizational setting.

## GENERIC SKILLS AND DISPOSITIONS

As outlined in Chapter One, the discussion about workforce skills emphasizes the need to improve generic skills and work-related dispositions over technical, job-specific skills.  Employers and many policymakers seem comfortable with the notion of generic skills and competencies and are able to describe what they desire of workers— abilities to solve problems, communicate effectively, work with others, take responsibility, work without supervision, and so on.

At present, there is no standard definition of generic skills, and the roles of general and context-specific knowledge in thinking is still a puzzling issue in social science.  Studies of expertise from a cognitive science perspective support findings from sociocultural studies and suggest that general skills do not take the place of domain-specific knowledge, nor do they operate exactly the same way from domain to domain.  Rather, specific applications of the general need to configure to the context (see Perkins and Salomon, 1989).

In this study, we began with a conception of generic skills developed in our previous research (Stasz et al., 1990; Stasz et al., 1993).  We defined two broad categories of generic skills:  basic or enabling skills, such as reading and simple mathematics; and complex reasoning skills, used to solve both formal and everyday problems encountered at school or work.  We also included work-related attitudes or dispositions, such as cooperative skills or personal qualities (e.g., responsibility, sociability) that can affect learning and performance on the job.  This conceptualization is similar to the widely accepted three-part foundation skills identified by SCANS (1991).

The focus of the analysis reported here is on problem solving, communications, teamwork, and work-related dispositions.  We emphasize these areas over others because of the general consensus that these capabilities are lacking in the workforce and that improving them requires public policy action. Several new studies indicate that these general skills are important to employers and workers. The NCEQW survey (1995) shows that employers place high value on general skills: employers rate applicant attitude and communication skills as the two most important factors in hiring new nonsupervisory production workers. Cappelli and Rogowsky (1995) surveyed workers and supervisors about the importance of skills (as defined by SCANS, 1991), their contribution to job performance, and the relationship between new systems of work organization and skill requirements. Employees ranked thinking skills (problem solving) first, followed by "ability to work with others," communication skills (speaking, listening, writing), and "ability to work in teams." Supervisor ratings largely overlapped those of workers.

This emphasis builds on our previous research but also takes some new directions. Our initial studies examined how generic skills and work-related attitudes could be taught to high school students in academic and vocational classrooms. It focused on how teachers can design learning environments that would, for example, help students learn to solve problems, collaborate with others, and take responsibility for their learning (Stasz et al., 1990, 1993). The present research examines these capabilities in the context of work, from the perspective of workers and employers, and draws more on recent literature on sociocultural aspects of work and on noncognitive factors in learning and performance.

## Problem Solving at Work

Discussions of skill needs in the changing workplace predict a shift in decisionmaking and problem solving from the supervisory level to the shop floor, where workers must cope on the spot with a growing number of unpredictable problems (Berryman and Bailey, 1992). Knowledge and skills are useful to the extent that workers can apply them to real problems and situations that they face at work.

Studies of cognition from a symbolic processing approach examine how problems are symbolically represented and manipulated; they often yield detailed analyses of problem characteristics, such as start states, goal states, constraints, and operators (e.g., Anderson, 1983; Newell and Simon, 1972). These studies are limited for our purposes because they typically study well-defined problems in laboratory or artificial settings rather than in real work contexts. Problems at work tend to be ill-defined, often unrecognized as problems, and have many possible solutions and solution methods (Lave, 1988). The research also typically focuses on individuals, and ignores social aspects of problem solving.

For the purposes of this study, we are interested in characterizing problem solving as it broadly defines work practice in each job, rather than providing a detailed breakdown of knowledge or procedures used to solve particular problems encountered (e.g., repairing a machine or diagnosing a patient's symptom). These broad themes should reflect the collaborative or interactive aspects of the work and the situated nature of problem-solving activities.

## Teamwork

Many discussions of new skill requirements in the workforce mention teamwork as a necessary skill. The SCANS (1991, 1992) reports, for example, list "participates as a member of a team" as an interpersonal competency. Others argue that the changing workplace puts a premium on teamwork and the ability of team members to cope with unpredictable problems (Berryman and Bailey, 1992).

As Darrah (1992) points out, teamwork is not a "skill" but a description of how work is organized. What constitutes a team is subject to local definition and thus must be defined in relation to the working context. Thus, the "skill" or "interpersonal competency" needed to participate in a team will depend on the work organization.

The organizational behavior literature provides some relevant definitions. Hackman and Oldham's (1980) classical work, for example, distinguishes between self-managing and co-acting work groups. A self-managing work group is an intact and definable social system, with a defined piece of work and authority to manage the task on its own. Self-managing work teams are also called autonomous work groups, semi-autonomous work groups, self-regulating work teams, or simply work teams (Levine and Moreland, 1991). In co-acting groups, individuals may report to the same supervisor and work close to one another, but they have individually defined tasks (Hackman and Oldham, 1980).

Sociocultural literature has looked at the culture of work groups and the reasons why work is often socially distributed, rather than individual. An important research question concerns the optimal distribution of knowledge in work groups and how the conditions in which the group works and the nature of the actions it must take shape knowledge distribution (e.g., Levine and Moreland, 1991; Hutchins, 1991). Other studies examine the processes by which newcomers become members of work groups or communities of practice (e.g., Levine and Moreland, 1992; Lave and Wenger, 1991).

Our analysis first examines the organization of work and then discusses implications for participation in particular work organizations.

## Communications

Communications skills are widely cited as among the most important skills needed by today's workers. As mentioned above, a recent national survey of employers identified communication as an important factor in making hiring decisions (NCEQW, 1995). A similar emphasis on communications skills appears in the SCANS framework. Four of the five foundation "basic skills" identified by SCANS are communications skills—the linguistic communications skills of reading, writing, speaking, and listening. Moreover, other components of the SCANS framework, including "personal qualities" such as amicable self-presentation and "workplace competencies" such as interpersonal skills and information utilization, also imply the need for strong communication skills (SCANS, *Learning a Living*, p. xiv).

Communications is a broad term that can be ambiguous. Unfortunately, this ambiguity is seldom taken into account when discussing communication skills on the job. Few would disagree, for example, that individuals who deal with the public (e.g., salespersons, flight attendants) may need different communications skills than more solitary workers, yet few discussions about communication skills make specific distinctions about how communication needs might vary from job to job.

Here we adopt a traditional analysis of communications that focuses on four axes: *audience*, or who is communicated with; *purpose*, why they are communicated with; *style*, the way in which the communicator presents himself or herself;[1] and *mode*, the means by which the communication is accomplished.[2] In addition to being familiar to instructors and trainers who may want to draw on our findings, this framework has the advantage of focusing on the situated nature of skills.

As we describe how the employees in our study actually communicated on the job, we will attend to the common distinction between using speech and text, but we will still consider both together, as does the SCANS framework. This is appropriate from several perspectives. In practice, these two kinds of skills are often used for communicating with similar purposes and audiences, and they may be used both in combination with and as a substitute for each other. (That is, communication through writing may often be used to supplement or to substitute for speaking, and vice versa.) Moreover, skills with spoken and with written language share a core of linguistic expertise that makes them amenable to related theoretical description and similar instructional strategies.

## Dispositions and Attitudes

In the skills debate, much attention has been paid to the dispositions and attitudes needed to succeed on the job. Some studies suggest that the skills gap identified by employers may be more about attitudes than academic or technical skills (Cappelli, 1992; Cappelli and Ianozzi, 1995). While survey data indicate that employers value "attitudes" (Natriello, 1989; NCEQW, 1995), it is not clear what they mean by this. Some employers may seek workers who have initiative, whereas others might want workers who follow orders.

Other studies of employers' perceptions of noncognitive skills attempt to distinguish different characteristics, such as "personal traits" and "social skills" (Bikson and Law, 1994) or "motivation" and "prosocial behavior" (Cappelli, 1992). Similarly, surveys of workers indicate that workers perceive noncognitive factors (e.g., dedication, resourcefulness) as essential for skilled work (Billett, 1993). Although

---

[1] In rhetorical theory, this axis is often referred to as *ethos*.

[2] On the history and applications of this framework, see James L. Kinneavy, *A Theory of Discourse: The Aims of Discourse*, New York: W. W. Norton, 1971, p. 18 ff.

surveys asking about skills—cognitive or noncognitive—provide evidence of general trends, the answers do not reveal what characteristics workers really have or how they play out in actual work situations (Darrah, 1992).

Theoretical work on the interplay of cognitive and other factors in learning and performance is still in development. Relevant psychological theories examine such factors as volition (Corno, 1993), motivation (Dweck and Leggett, 1988; Dweck and Elliot, 1983), and dispositions (Prawat, 1989; Perkins, Jay, and Tishman, 1993a, b) as individual traits, yet recognize that situational context plays a role in shaping them. If context plays a role and traits are not static, then understanding noncognitive factors is important for public policy. Actions to develop positive dispositions toward work through education and training make sense only if they can be shaped (Cappelli, 1992).

Volition—paying attention to and working toward appropriate goals—is described by adjectives such as conscientiousness, disciplined, self-directed, resourceful, and striving. Volition directs intellectual and emotional energy to achieving goals, especially when the situation calls for it (e.g., if the task is difficult and there are distractions) (Corno, 1993).

Motivations account for the discrepancy between what individuals can do and what they actually do. Research distinguishes between "mastery" or "performance" orientations toward learning (Dweck and Leggett, 1988; Dweck and Elliott, 1983). A mastery approach seeks challenging tasks and persists under failure; it correlates with constructive views of ability, feelings of efficacy and confidence, and efficiency in complex learning situations. Individuals with a performance orientation are more concerned with how they might look to others than with what they might learn; this can influence how they value a task and the effort they put into it.

Dispositions or "habits of mind" are individuals' tendencies to put their capabilities into action and are thought to influence how individuals deal with various situations (Prawat, 1989; Perkins, Jay, and Tishman, 1993a). Dispositions are essential for performance because "unless one has the inclination to use it, ability will lay fallow" (Perkins, Jay, and Tishman, 1993a).

Perkins and his colleagues propose a dispositional theory of good thinking—defined as flexible, insightful, or productive thinking—which complements current views of the kind of thinking skills called for in the changing workplace. Dispositions have three components: inclination (the felt tendency toward behavior X), sensitivity (alertness to X occasions), and ability (ability to follow through with X behavior) (Perkins, Jay, and Tishman, 1993b). This perspective acknowledges that dispositions are grounded in belief systems, values, and attitudes, are culturally based, and are thus acquired through a process of acculturation. By observing and living within a particular culture, individuals gradually start to adopt the behavior and belief systems of the culture (Perkins et al., 1993; Brown, Collins, and Duguid, 1989).

Theoretical constructs like volition, motivation, and disposition are primarily psychological, have focused on learning in academic or laboratory settings, and have barely explored sociocultural influences. Thus they provide only an initial starting point for examining the meaning of dispositions in work settings. Because the concept of dispositions appears to subsume both motivation and volition, we used this term in our analysis.

## INSTITUTIONAL RESPONSES TO CHANGING SKILL NEEDS

Because a primary motivation for studying skills at work is the widespread belief that skills are changing, it is important to assess employers' views on skill demands and their responses to changing demands, including the local forces and economic conditions that shape them (Grubb et al., 1992; Darrah, 1992). At the institutional or workplace level, research on organizational change and organizational productivity suggests several themes to examine. Employers can respond to perceived skill demands in several ways, including hiring employees with certain skills, producing skills in their own training programs, or creating incentives that encourage workers to invest in their own skills. In addition to creating new skill capabilities, appropriate work design and human resource policies must be in place to achieve better performance results (Finegold, 1991; Bailey, 1993b). Once an organization adopts a strategy for acquiring the skills it needs, the quality of the implementation process—the decisions and actions that translate ideas and policies into day-today practices—is key to reaching successful outcomes (Bikson, Gutek, and Mankin, 1981; Bikson and Eveland, 1991).

To determine employer responses to changing skill needs, we gathered data to answer several questions. How do employers view their skill needs, given the changes their organization or industry faces? What policies do they establish to meet their needs, including selection, hiring, and training practices? Are their decisions linked to the firm's business strategy or organizational mission? Or are they influenced by union rules or other factors? Are their policies effective? Our analysis includes informal and structured on-the-job training in addition to formal training and, in particular, the role of the community of practice in assimilating newcomers and providing training. We also examine other policies that can affect skill development, such as the existence of career paths and unionization.

## THE FIELD STUDY

We conducted the field study in three overlapping phases—site selection, worksite observations and interviews, and analysis. We used a multisite, replicated case study design in which similar sets of criteria were used to select participating firms and individuals within them, and in which common data gathering procedures were employed across the sites. This conceptual approach lends itself to a case study research design that is particularly appropriate for examining and interpreting ongoing processes in real-world contexts, especially when the processes to be studied (work processes or approaches to training or recruitment) are not sharply separable from their contexts and when the variables of interest are likely to outnumber the units of study (Yin, 1994). We next detail our research and analysis methods and define the variables of interest. Table 2.1 illustrates the data sources.

### Sample Selection

We were interested in sites that were experiencing changes affecting the skill demands of frontline workers in their subbaccalaureate labor force and were willing to cooperate with the research demands of the study (interviewing several levels of management; observing and

## Table 2.1

### Data Sources

| Classes of Variables | Source | | | | |
| --- | --- | --- | --- | --- | --- |
| | Telephone Interview | In-Person Interview | Cognitive Task Analysis | Observation | Document |
| Worker skills and dispositions | | X | X | X | X |
| Community of practice/work organization | X | X | X | X | |
| Organization characteristics (e.g., size, product, ownership) | X | X | | | X |
| Organization mission/vision/management strategy | X | X | | | X |
| Perceptions of skill needs | X | X | X | | X |
| Responses to skill needs (e.g., hiring, selection, training, change strategies) | | X | | X | X |
| Worksite connections to schools | X | X | | | |

interacting with frontline workforce on the job). The subbaccalaureate labor force—the labor market for those with less than a baccalaureate degree but at least a high school diploma—was of particular interest for several reasons: It constitutes about three-fifths of the labor market; it has been growing steadily in the last decade, as have the community colleges and technical institutes that prepare occupational students; and it is poorly understood with respect to the relationship between formal schooling and subsequent employment

(Grubb et al., 1992). It is also intensely local—subject to cyclical variation in the local economy, which can undermine incentives to accumulate extensive training and experience, and dominated by informal methods for searching for employment and hiring new workers (Grubb and McDonnell, 1991; Grubb et al., 1992). While the subbaccalaureate market encompasses a wide range of jobs across all job categories, our focus is on craft and technical jobs, rather than low-paying jobs often associated with a service economy (e.g., in fast-food restaurants and clerical pools).[3]

To identify sites and occupational categories in the greater Los Angeles area labor market, we sought information and examined data from several sources. We obtained local data on job demands to identify occupations currently in demand and likely to grow in the coming decades.   Data from the Economic Development Department on projections of employment in Los Angeles County from 1990–1997 indicated an average growth rate for all occupations of about 5.7 percent.  Since growth was expected in virtually every sector of the economy—the exception being manufacturing in the high tech/aerospace segments—we examined projections for the fastest growing occupations to help define the potential sample. Another reason to study "in demand" jobs is that these jobs are likely to have organizational support because of their value to a firm.

We employed a "snowballing" or "chain-sampling" approach to locate potential sites (see Patton, 1980). We contacted firms throughout metropolitan Los Angeles based on leads from a school-business collaborative operating locally and other professional contacts.  In addition, we visited several community colleges that engage in a variety of workforce development programs, such as contract training for local employers and retraining for displaced workers. From these sources, we developed a list of potential candidate firms and began a process of first contacting firms to gauge their interest in being part of the study. Altogether, we contacted nine firms over six months.

----
[3]Service occupations have remained relatively stable: from 1900–1988 service occupations grew only 4 percent (Barley, 1995). Furthermore, skill requirements for these jobs are less likely to be affected by the changes we have discussed, except to further differentiate them from occupations where technical skills are at a premium.

The selection process involved several steps, including a telephone interview, meetings with management to negotiate study approval, and meetings to identify target departments and workers. Within the targeted department, we identified experienced and less-experienced workers to observe and interview. The final study sample included four sites and seven jobs, as shown in Table 2.2. The sites represent both service and manufacturing sectors, and vary by size, unionization, and other characteristics. Chapter Three describes sites and jobs in more detail.[4]

## Worksite Observations

Site visits occurred over about one week, with some returns to accommodate study participants' schedules. Worksite observations covered three aspects of work common across all jobs: a start-up period, everyday routines, and everyday relations with others. We

**Table 2.2**

**Study Sites and Target Jobs**

| Site | Target Job |
|------|-----------|
| Transportation agency (TA) | Construction inspector<br>Survey inspector |
| Health care agency (HA) | Licensed vocational nurse<br>Home health aide |
| Microprocessor manufacturing (MPM) | Test technician<br>Equipment technician |
| Traffic management (TM) | Traffic signal technician |

---

[4]Because the jobs finally selected do not necessarily match available public data, and because firms do not always back up their perceived job demands with hard data (e.g., the transportation agency), we do not have demand data for all the jobs in the sample. The available data on target occupations with the largest absolute growth show 15.8 percent growth from 1990–1997 for licensed vocational nurses and 39.1 percent growth for home health care workers. Industry data for the same period show 2.6 percent growth for electronic equipment manufacturing (test cell and equipment technicians) and 7.7 percent growth for all construction, with construction trade occupations increasing 6.3 percent (construction and survey inspectors belong to this subgroup). (Source: *Occupational Outlook Handbook, 1992–93 Edition*, U.S. Department of Labor, Bureau of Labor Statistics, May 1992.)

employed Spradley's (1980) framework for understanding social settings as an organizing guide for fieldworkers' questions, observations, and fieldnotes. The social setting framework includes the following dimensions: space, actors, acts, activities, events, objects, goals, time, and feeling. Trained fieldworkers were asked to include holistic observations about everyday routines, relations, and work start-up in their daily fieldnotes.

Since jobs are socially organized and physically situated in particular ways, we developed study plans for jobs that fit particular conditions. For jobs that convene experienced and new workers in a common space and assign specific tasks, we expected that one observer could accomplish observation in two days. Only the equipment technician job (at MPM) fell within this class. On the first day, the fieldworker had a brief tour and work orientation, followed by observation of everyday routine. For fairly routine assigned tasks, each task was observed on the average of 8–10 times. Then the fieldworker focused on everyday relations involved to accomplish tasks (i.e., the people involved, their positions in the firm, and their relationship to tasks.) On day two, the fieldworker observed tasks and relationships required to initiate work at the beginning of the work day.

When jobs involved teaming, we revised the approach to include an additional half-day to observe the team's routines and relations. The test cell technicians and survey inspectors fell into this class of work.

When jobs required workers to be highly mobile or itinerant, we studied the job over three days, traveling with frontline workers during that time. The travel time permitted informal interviews with frontline workers about tasks and work context. Construction inspector, home health aide, licensed vocational nurse, and traffic signal technician jobs fell within this classification.

For all observations, we sought to observe enough workers to cover the critical tasks assigned to a job and to witness the job performed by at least one newcomer and two to three experienced workers. After the observation phase, fieldworkers conducted formal interviews with frontline workers and department supervisors (discussed below).

Because of our relatively short time at worksites and because the jobs we selected are technical and in some cases require licenses and certifications to perform, we did not undertake participant observation. Rather, we depended on our worker informants to articulate their understanding of the work and tasks.

## Formal Interviews

We conducted two types of formal semi-structured interviews.  The first interview covered dimensions of the work context, including the organization, vision, and mission, products and services, staffing and training investments, skill and attitude requirements, productivity improvements, change strategies, and perceptions about workers and their concerns.  We probed these aspects of work context across classes of participants, including top managers, high-level contractors and consultants, human resources officers, trainers, middle managers, department supervisors, frontline workers, and key professionals who support department activities.[5]  Supervisor and frontline worker interviews also asked about respondents' education and training histories.  Each audiotaped interview required one to one and one-half hours.  Table 2.3 shows interviews conducted at each worksite.

The second type of semi-structured formal interview inquired about tasks involved in the frontline job.  This cognitive task analysis (CTA) was meant to elicit specific task dimensions:  production rules, production processes, mental models, and images.  Results from the CTA are presented separately (see unpublished manuscript by Black et al., 1995) and includes data from the CTA about worker attitudes and dispositions.

## Document Collection

To gather additional data, we attempted to collect the following documents systematically across firms:  organization charts, employee

---

[5]Although our study design called for participation by union leadership, we were not successful in accomplishing this.  Three of the seven frontline jobs we studied were represented by a local union.  In two cases, the workers described their union as bargaining units to preserve pay and benefits for a wide range of workers.  In the third case (home health), the union leadership did not return our calls requesting interviews, even though they had expressed interest in participating.

### Table 2.3

### Interviews by Worksite

| Level | TA | MPM | TM | HA |
|---|---|---|---|---|
| Executive | 2 | 2 | 1 | 1 |
| Human resources | 2 | 2 | | 1 |
| Manager | 4 | 1 | 1 | 1 |
| Trainer | 1 | 1 | 7[a] | 1 |
| Staff professional | 1 | | | 1 |
| Supervisor | 2 | 2 | 1 | 1 |
| Frontline worker[b] | 4 | 4 | 4 | 3 |

[a]Includes one individual interview and two group interviews, representing three agencies overall.

[b]Interview and cognitive task analysis questions for each.

benefit packages, annual reports, employee evaluation forms and procedures, company newsletters, syllabi for training programs, and procedures used by frontline workers to perform tasks.

## Analytic Procedures

Following procedures developed in our earlier research (Stasz et al., 1993), the analytic phase of the field study involved an iterative process of indexing observational data, domain analysis, and generation of themes. We developed index categories that corresponded with the dimensions of work context used to structure the formal interviews, and on other study goals (e.g., worksite connection to schools). As fieldwork commenced, we built on the initial domains by adding categories that emerged at different sites.

Fieldworkers coded interviews and observation notes, which were entered into a computer program for managing text data. To achieve reliability in coding, each fieldworker indexed several sets of fieldnotes and interviews written by other fieldworkers. As a group, the study team compared results, clarified definitions, and identified any missing categories.

Once our preliminary analysis was completed, we returned to each worksite to debrief the study participants on our interpretations of the results and preliminary findings. The debriefing provided a validity check for our findings and gave study participants the opportunity to discuss the implications of the findings for their worksite.

## LIMITATIONS OF THE STUDY

The perceptions and behaviors of the respondents in this study's sample may not generalize to all job incumbents, managers, and worksites in similar occupational areas. Indeed, because of the situated nature of skills and dispositions and because of expected variations in organizational responses to skill development needs and issues, we did not aim for generalizability in the statistical sense. However, the triangulation method and debriefings to the firms did help provide validity checks of respondents' answers to surveys and fieldworkers' observations.

The jobs and worksites were selected because they represent technical work in the subbaccalaureate labor market in organizations facing changing skill demands. Such organizations are thus likely to have grappled with the questions at hand: the relevance and importance of generic skills and dispositions in work, organizational responses to acquiring and developing skills, and employers' connections with education providers as a way to identify potential technical workers and to assist incumbent workers' skill development. The study can provide rich information to other organizations facing changes that affect their skill demands and to educational providers attempting to improve youth preparation for work.

# Chapter Three

# TECHNICAL WORK IN FOUR FIRMS

## OVERVIEW OF FOUR FIRMS

This chapter provides an overview of the firms we studied and descriptions of the work that took place in them by the workers we observed.

As we indicated in the previous chapter, our final study sample included sites in four firms that represent different business areas: a transportation agency (TA), a traffic management agency (TM), a microprocessor manufacturer (MPM), and a health care agency (HA).[1] Table 3.1 summarizes their key characteristics. As the table indicates, the size of the firms, in terms of personnel, range from 26 people to tens of thousands. Two firms, TM and TA, are public agencies, whereas the other two are private sector businesses.

The sites have very different product or customer bases—three have service functions; one (MPM) is a product manufacturer. They serve markets of varying scale, from local (TM), to regional (TA), national (HA), and international (MPM).

A salient issue for firms and for many of the workers we observed was that most of these sites were feeling the pinch of austerity: two sites had recently undergone staffing reductions, and in TM and HA the threat of having services outsourced to contractors was felt strongly

---

[1]Individual study respondents and participating firms were assured anonymity; all proper names appearing in this report are pseudonyms. We conducted interviews at three traffic management agencies and observed technicians in one of them.

**Table 3.1**

**Overview of Firms**

| Characteristic | Transportation Agency | Traffic Management | Microprocessor Manufacturing | Health Care Agency |
|---|---|---|---|---|
| Number of employees based in region | 8,000 | 26 | 650 | 33,000 |
| Ownership | Public agency | Public agency | Publicly traded | Publicly traded |
| Fiscal and operational autonomy from parent firm | Fiduciary agency: holds the purse strings and controls contracts | Operating unit of city government | Operating unit of multi-national corporation | Operating unit of national hospital chain |
| Product/ customers | Transportation planning and programming; operating bus system; and construction of rail, streets, and highway systems | Increased mobility, reducing urban congestion | Manufacture and sell over 4,000 different semiconductor switches | Health maintenance and acute care; site customers older, with higher acuity; multilingual |
| Market | Regional | Local | International | Domestic |
| Vision | Deliver coordinated transportation service and improve air quality; help people get out of cars while ensuring adequate mobility in the region | Maintain safety of the motoring public: "How many times do you see a green light and think 'oh well, I better stop because it might be green the other way?' . . . a trust that you have to keep" | Be a world leader in semiconductors and deliver strong investor returns; provide a good working environment and contribute to society by using technology to save energy | Provide quality health care in the most cost-effective way, with greater satisfaction; home care is going to be one of the ways to reduce hospital costs and improve quality of care |

Table 3.1—continued

|  | Transportation Agency | Traffic Management | Microprocessor Manufacturing | Health Care |
|---|---|---|---|---|
| Fiscal performance/ strategy | Investment/austerity | Austerity | Investment/profit | Austerity |
| Unionized | Yes | Yes | No | Yes |
| Productivity improvements | Establishing consortia with other transit agencies; using TQM at senior levels to manage budget cuts while raising efficiency | Transition from "wires and pliers" to electronics; signals all computerized and controlled from downtown | Systemwide goal to link plants worldwide; 5 percent of budget allocated to R&D; using team-based manufacturing "cells," training managers, engineers, and technicians in cross-functional teams | Top-down programs in TQM and CQI; use teams to create learning organization; database and finance systems to identify best practices, create standards, and innovate |
| Worksite connections to local schools | Programs with local high schools geared to transportation-related careers (architecture, engineering, and urban planning) | None; "in-house" training program; urge new staff to work on two-year degree along with training session | None; member of a school/ business coalition; generally hire from specific community college or training programs | Health academy program in local high schools; worker retraining and clinical placement programs with community colleges |

by the frontline workers. Of the four firms, only MPM is not unionized.

Added to these financial pressures were the substantial attempts to improve productivity that all sites were trying to implement. Almost all the workers we observed were facing rapid changes in technology and in the way their work was done. Three firms had begun using new management practices such as total quality management (TQM), continuous quality improvement (CQI), or organizational learning to guide restructuring of many aspects of their operations.

Finally, as the final row of the table indicates, the two smallest firms, TM and MPM, have no formal connections to schools, whereas the two larger firms, TA and HA, have been proactive in establishing these connections, largely through links with local high schools.

In all, we examined seven jobs in detail: traffic signal technicians working in the TM agency; home health aides and licensed vocational nurses (LVNs) in the HA; test cell associates and equipment technicians in the MPM firm; and construction inspectors and survey inspectors at the TA. In the remainder of this chapter, we describe the seven jobs that we observed at these four firms. These scenarios are based on data gathered from observations, interviews, and documents collected at the sites. They are intended to convey a picture of the job in the larger contexts of work and organization.

## MANAGING TRAFFIC

From all appearances, the maintenance yard of the Department of Public Works seems similar to yards in any other medium-sized city in the United States—men and women in brown and orange uniforms walk among maintenance sheds labeled as sanitation, street maintenance, electrical, and carpentry shops. Sanitation vehicles, a variety of pickup trucks, and a few covered electric carts sit in the lot. A mix of office personnel and line staff stand in the middle of the yard chatting amiably while going through stretching exercises designed to reduce back injuries.

This image changes almost immediately, however, when one enters the offices of the traffic signal maintenance unit. The first room one sees on entering this shed is the "Traffic Control Room." Through the glass panel in the door, one can see the computers, video monitors, and communications equipment that are crowded into the small room—a mix of high technology that seems out of place in this setting. And there is only one reason this traffic signal unit has this technology—Sam Burns, the director of the unit.

Sam, who is in his mid-50s, is dressed in a button-down shirt with a faded tie. Both a beeper and a walkie-talkie are attached to his belt. He is happy to offer interested parties a short tour of the "traffic surveillance" system that enables him to monitor most of the intersections in the downtown area. Two large monitors display video images of traffic movement along the main roadway through town. A computer terminal in another corner shows activity as the signals at an intersection go through their phases, controlling traffic flows and pedestrian crossing patterns in four directions. These signals are sent to the control room from microprocessor-based controllers located at each intersection. These units not only control the timing of the lights at the intersection, but communicate with the central control room via a network of coaxial and fiber-optic cables that connect almost all the intersections in the downtown area of the city.

Rapid changes in information and communications technology have led to a silent revolution under and above the streets, fundamentally changing the demands facing traffic signal technicians in this unit. Sam switches the video display to show another intersection, where magnetic signal "loops" embedded in the roadway have been replaced by programmable video detectors that change signals when vehicles pull up to the intersection. The traffic signal unit is working with manufacturers as a "beta" test site for this new technology, which has been installed at two intersections in the city. Sam proudly explains the even newer technology that the unit has begun using: miniature microwave transmitters to communicate among controllers in the network, cellular communications to download "timing patterns" from the central computer system to controllers in the field, and even radar and sonar devices to monitor the speed and density of traffic flow.

The differences between this technological wonderland and the day-to-day reality of traffic signal maintenance are unveiled almost immediately after one leaves the signal control room and enters the shop.  Dusty shelves piled high with spare red, yellow, and green traffic signal gels, pedestrian crossing buttons, wiring harnesses, and other hardware reach to the ceiling.  A large four-way "auto head" runs through red, yellow, and green phases from its perch on a mounting pole in the middle of the floor.  Two new aluminum cabinets containing all the electronics used at an intersection stand nearby, running through tests that ensure their proper operation before they are placed in the field.  Two signal technicians sit at work benches, a variety of electronic units open before them as they work on testing and repairing damaged devices.  Units too old or too damaged to be repaired sit on shelves atop these work areas.  One of the techs says, "you never know when you might be able to use something" in these units.  The dust covering the pile of units indicates that they have not been used in a long time.

Out in the field, Mark, an experienced technician, notes a head that has been knocked out of alignment.  He points out that trucks pass through this intersection on their way to the harbor, and it has only eight-foot lanes that are difficult for big trucks to negotiate.  As a result, trucks bang into the signals hanging at the corner, forcing him to return to this intersection many times to repair the signal.  The problem could be averted by a slightly wider lane, but he feels the engineers are not going to listen to him.

Mark pulls the truck up to the corner under the misaligned light and turns on the yellow warning flashers.  He sets out six orange traffic cones behind and next to the truck.  He pulls on his chest harness and removes several tools from the tool bin on the right side of the truck—a socket wrench, some light bulbs, and a large, specialized wrench.  He places the bulbs and tools in the bottom of a bucket attached to a boom on the back of the truck, and climbs aboard.  After attaching a safety line, he moves the boom to a spot adjacent to the signal using the controls located on the end of the boom arm.

Mark first turns the light to its proper orientation.  He turns the wing nuts on the edge of the cover, and opens the top and bottom lights. He cleans the lens and reflectors within the light and changes the bulbs.  Using his hands, he bends the twisted sheet metal backplate on the signal back into a reasonably straight shape.  Finally, using the special wrench he tightens the top and bottom bolts on the light. Mark moves the boom next to the other auto head on the pole and repeats the cleaning and bulb changing procedure he did on the first signal.

This is a very busy intersection, near the entry to the harbor. The two roads have six and five lanes, respectively. Traffic moves by at almost highway speeds, and the majority of vehicles seem to be medium-sized and large trucks. The whoosh of buses, trucks, and honking horns is overwhelming. It is a loud, dusty, and very gritty corner. The smells from the harbor, the oil refinery, and a nearby garbage-burning power plant are strong, and seem remote from the high-tech wizardry we saw back at the shop.

## CARING FOR PATIENTS AT HOME

Irene Simmons walks up to the door on the first floor of a small apartment building and rings the bell. After a few moments, a frail voice calls, "Irene, is that you?" and the patient opens the door to let us in. As a LVN who works for a home health care agency in Los Angeles, Irene has visited this patient once or twice a week since his discharge from the hospital two months ago. Even without meeting her, one would immediately know that Irene is a nurse, as much from her terse but nurturing manner as from the white coat, identification badge, and stethoscope she wears. The patient is in his late 60s and has been diagnosed with end-stage AIDS. His home is cluttered, somewhat dark, and stuffy. Near his bed in the living room sit a number of small tables piled high with pill boxes, tissue dispensers, blankets, and medical supplies. A television plays loudly in the corner—the patient makes a point of telling us that he watches the news, never the soaps. While he is quite coherent, he is clearly a fragile, ailing man.

Irene visits this patient to monitor his condition. She begins by asking him a series of questions about his appetite, drinking, bowel movement, urination, and sleeping patterns. She helps him to a scale to measure his weight, supporting him so he will not lose his balance as he steps up onto the machine. She compliments him on having continued to gain weight—his inability to do so is the primary reason the nursing case manager, Kathy Carlson, has had a nurse continue visits on a regular basis. Irene uses a blood pressure cuff to check the patient's blood pressure, makes certain that his pill boxes are filled for each day in the next two weeks, and tells him that she is sorry to see an ashtray filled with cigarette butts in his living room—smoking is very bad for a person in his condition.  After washing her hands, Irene thanks the patient and reminds him that she will be returning early next week for another visit.

When we go to her car, Irene says it is usually filled with files and nursing supplies that she needs in the field.  She normally spends much of her day alone driving around the city.  As she drives to the second of five homes she is scheduled to visit this day, her beeper goes off.  While she would like to have a portable phone that would allow her to respond immediately to her supervisor, the home health agency does not provide them and she might not want to carry such a valuable item into some of the neighborhoods she has to visit.  Instead, she will use the phone at the next patient's home.

Another staff person from the home health agency has arrived at this home ten minutes earlier.  Sue Perkins is a home health aide (HHA) whose main responsibility is bathing patients.  The patient is already in her bathrobe and ready for her shower, so Irene tells Sue she will wait until they are done and use the time to call Kathy and get a start on some of her paperwork ("charting").  Irene notes that it is not uncommon for her to run into other members of the treatment team who work with these patients.  When a patient is referred to the home care agency, a registered nurse (RN) conducts an assessment visit, identifying needed services for each patient.  A single case can have four or more service providers assigned, including RNs, LVNs, HHAs, social workers, and physical, occupational, or speech therapists.  If a service is needed and the agency has no staff available to provide the service, the case manager will arrange with the intake unit to have an outside contract agency provide that service.

While Irene makes her calls, Sue has helped the patient into the bathroom.  The patient is in her early 70s, has pronounced surgical scars on her chest, and has just had her left leg amputated below the knee.  After placing a bath bench in the shower and making certain it is stable, Sue turns the water on and warms the seat.  The patient moves next to the bench and, with Sue's assistance, lifts herself out of the chair and onto the bench.  Sue notes that while it can be difficult to have to lift and move some patients, this patient has been well trained in moving in and out of her chair by her physical therapist.  In addition to bathing the patient, Sue takes the opportunity to lead her through a series of range-of-motion exercises and checks her thoroughly for any marks or redness on the skin. Such marks can be signs of injury or even abuse. Sue will report any new marks to her case supervisor.

After Sue finishes helping the patient dress, she says good-bye and leaves. Irene moves quickly through her checkup of the patient, asking the same series of questions she asked at the first home and checking blood pressure. She also draws a small blood sample, which will be tested by the agency lab to ensure that the patient's medication is appropriate. The sample is placed in a small icebox to keep it cool until it reaches the lab. After checking the patient's pill box, she says good-bye and departs to the third patient's house, which is just a few blocks away.

The home health agency that Irene works for is reorganizing in ways intended to provide quality care at competitive prices. Like other health agencies around the country, it is shortening hospital stays for patients and increasing home health care. This change affects not only the training of home health care workers like Irene and Sue, but the balance and distribution of skills for the patient care team, which includes doctors, nurses, pharmacists, therapists, and other health professionals.

## MANUFACTURING ELECTRONIC COMPONENTS

The Microprocessor Manufacturing Corporation (MPM) is a mid-sized, specialized manufacturer of cutting-edge microchips. A family-owned firm that has been involved in the construction of electronic components used in military or space applications since the 1940s, MPM expects global sales to approach $1 billion by the end of this century. To reach this goal, the firm has built factories and distribution centers in the United States, Mexico, Europe, and Asia. More recently, it began implementing new approaches to structuring work in some units—approaches that reflect many of the latest management practices reported almost daily in the business press.

One unit that has received a great deal of attention in MPM is the Z1 Test Cell, a quality assurance unit that performs final testing and quality certification on some of the most complex chips MPM produces. The cell's work area is part of a larger work area crowded with test and finishing equipment that serves all cells responsible for final production of the most complex military and space-level microchips. Everyone in this "clean room" wears blue anti-static smocks and hair nets to protect the sensitive chips from static electric charges that could be damaging—failure of one chip could disable a multi-million-dollar satellite or piece of military equipment.

The Z1 cell team consists of four members:  two experienced technicians (Ng and Roger) and two relative newcomers to MPM (Tom and Prat).  This cell has largely taken the lead in implementing the new management practices that have been put in place in MPM over the last year.  Control charts showing statistical process control measures such as cycle time, throughput, work in progress, time in queue, and downtime cover a corkboard.  One-third of the space available in this work area is empty, following a recent redesign of the work area layout that identified the additional space as a factor in elevated cycle times.  When one asks any member of the team who the team leader is, he responds that decisions are made as a team and that no individual holds sway.  However, even a small amount of time spent in the unit reveals that these new practices may not have taken hold quite as deeply as it may seem at first.  Team members do not understand all the control charts that are posted.  When the supervisor needs something to be done, he approaches Ng with the problem, and relies on Ng to lead the team to a solution to the problem.

On a day-to-day basis, however, this is not a common event:  the work is steady and often repetitive.  Each member of the cell works independently, running different batches of chips through a sequence of tests specified in a "lot traveler" form.  Although the test sequences do vary by type of chip and customer demands set in contracts, they generally follow a similar flow.  Once the chips are drawn from the stockroom, they are mounted on aluminum test boards and run through high- and low-temperature cycling tests.  All aspects of their operation are then tested on the "DAC," an electronics testing machine that is so complex that it requires its own mini-computer.  Chips are then run through tests of the "source" (the output side of the chip) and "gate" (the input side of the chip), to ensure they can handle the voltages they are rated for.  Before chips run another cycle through the DAC, some lots (especially those to be used in space satellites) are run through a centrifuge test to see if they can handle physical stresses and an x-ray test to check for minute fractures. Despite these demanding tests, failure rates exceeding 2 percent were rare.

Although the members of the test cell have stronger technical backgrounds than many production workers in the unit, these differences emerge only in subtle situations. For example, one of the newer technicians (Tom) had, the day before, been trained to use a PIND tester, a piece of test equipment that was to be transferred to the new unit the following week. Although Ng had never used the equipment before, he was surprised at how long it was taking Tom to learn the equipment. Tom reported that he had, in fact, learned how to use the equipment in an hour, but that he had been trying to run a batch of chips through the tests and that these tests were long and labor-intensive—each chip had to run through the PIND tester five times, one chip at a time. This did not sound right to Ng, who checked the engineer's manual to see if this was the proper test procedure. It was not: chips had to go through the test only one time, unless the failure rate for a lot exceeded 2 percent. For Ng, solving these problems was one of the most enjoyable aspects of his job.

In another department at MPM, technicians are working on research and development of new chip processing technology. In this area, the men responsible for repair and maintenance of the machines are constantly on call to troubleshoot and repair machines that are down. Downtime can cost the company in terms of lost production, which places pressure on the technicians to perform rapid, yet thorough work. In addition, the chemicals and machinery used in this area can be quite dangerous—techs literally have the lives of other workers in their hands.

The team of technicians consists of six men who work two at a time, 24 hours a day. The senior equipment technician, Bob, has been at MPM for ten years, having come directly from high school. Since coming to MPM, he has completed an A.S. in Electrical Engineering and a B.S. in Manufacturing Engineering on his own time. He generally works independently, first checking the semiconductor productivity network (SPN) to see which machines are down, and then traveling around the "fab" (the room that houses the manufacturing equipment) working on various pieces of equipment. He is very efficient and deliberate in his actions—it is clear that he knows his machines and feels confident.  At the same time, he says he likes his job because there is always something new to learn with the changing technology.  The very nature of his job means that he is continually faced with new problems to solve when machines go down.

Bob also likes the diversity of responsibilities involved in the technician job, from performing equipment modifications and upgrades, cleaning and rebuilding parts, to designing out errors from the machines.  His job involves developing operating procedures for equipment, completing paperwork, and updating the status of his work on the computer through the SPN.  In addition, since Bob has a great deal of experience at MPM, he trains the new technicians.  Using a combination of lecturing, coaching, and hands-on demonstrations, he helps bring new and less-expert employees up to speed.

Bob keeps in constant communication with the staff operating the machines.  They all make quite an image as they move about the lab completely decked out in blue smocks, hoods, gloves, surgical masks, and boots (which are necessary to keep a completely sterile environment).  The operators approach Bob whenever machines are down or they want him to delay work on a machine.  In addition, the statistical processing information the operators provide to Bob helps him recognize and diagnose problems with the equipment, and determine repairs.  At lunch, Bob joins the operators in the break room.  All of the operators are female, while the technicians are male.  They spend the lunch hour chatting about various personal and work issues, such as the new work schedule being implemented by management so that the plant can operate 24 hours a day, seven days a week.  All but three of the 20 team members have volunteered to change their schedules.  They'll continue to get the same pay, but will work only 70 hours every two-week period instead of the traditional 80 hours.

Bob does not seem concerned about the upcoming change in schedule.  He takes it in stride, just as he takes the rest of his job.  His accommodating attitude helps him not only deal with, but enjoy the demands of his job.

## BUILDING A TRANSPORTATION SYSTEM

There may well be no more visible public project in Los Angeles than one that is going on underground: construction of a new subway system that will, over the next 30 years, cost an estimated $180 billion. With the unsteady southern California economy, this project has received substantial attention not only for its ability to meet the region's transportation needs, but in its role as a potential economic engine. It has also been subject to enormous attention from political actors and the media, who have frequently pointed out cost over-runs, design flaws, and questions regarding construction quality.

Any project the size, scope, and complexity of the Los Angeles subway system requires meticulous planning and substantial oversight. Whereas planning is the responsibility of a regional transportation agency (TA), three international construction firms are responsible for actually building the system. Between the TA and the contractors sit the project's contract managers: one engineering firm for each of the lines of the system is responsible for quality assurance by ensuring that the construction firms and thousands of subcontractors building the subway do so in strict accord with contract requirements. In essence, their goal is to "make sure the TA gets exactly what it is paying for." On a day-to-day basis, this work on the subway line falls to construction inspectors, who spend each day on the construction site.

Ten teams of inspectors are assigned to different sites snaking along the TA's Yellow Line construction project. These teams are responsible for making certain that all aspects of the construction process—including excavating tunnels and stations, pouring concrete walls, installing electrical, plumbing, and communications systems, laying track, and restoring streets after construction—are completed properly. The breadth of these tasks requires inspection teams made up of highly experienced staff, each of whom has a different specialization. These areas of expertise are reflected in the makeup of one team, which was based near the station under construction at the intersection of Main Street and Fifth Avenue near downtown Los Angeles. The four members of the team have surprisingly similar backgrounds—all have pursued some college education (engineering, architecture, or design), but only one has a degree. All have extensive experience in construction, and most have worked on large projects before—freeway construction, mining projects, or international construction. Each has a unique specialty: Sidney, the lead inspector, has a background in design and as a manager of his family's construction company; Paul is a communications and electrical specialist; Andy's expertise is in metallurgy and excavation; and Rex specializes in mining and mechanical units.

The team's offices are crowded and functional—the four inspectors have their drafting desks right up against one another. Each desk is layered with plans, production schedules, and progress reports. Two large blueprint stands and a tall metal rack (piled with hard hats, flashlights, safety glasses, and several new red safety vests) stand against the walls. No computers are in evidence. Walls are papered with plans of the station under construction nearby, including cross-sectional maps of the station without walls, a map of the tunnel, a construction schedule, and a milestone chart. A small sign over one of the drafting tables says "Arguing with an inspector is like wrestling with a pig in the mud. After a while, you realize the pig enjoys it."

The construction site is located across the street from the team's offices. Surrounded by a chain link fence, the site stretches a full city block and more than four stories underground. Although a compressor and cranes operate at ground level, the site is surprisingly quiet—traffic has been diverted around this block, creating an oasis of calm in the heart of the city. This situation has generated vehement complaints from local merchants, who fear losing their businesses before the construction is completed. Sidney has suggested that the team do as much shopping as possible at these stores, as a small gesture to help the owners. One enters the work area via an ill-shapen wooden ladder that allows you to climb ten feet down onto the roof of the station shell. At this point, there are no internal walls in place, and one can only imagine where the tracks will run and where the elevators, staircases, and token booths will be placed. The most important worksite today is on the third level down in the structure, where crews are working rapidly to build a concrete wall. It is cold, wet, and dusty in the completely enclosed space: the only illumination comes from several lights powered by two small, noisy generators. Approximately 30 men (there are no women working in this area) are working on the wall.

Electrical workers are moving feverishly around the work space: two workers are "tied off" 30 feet above the floor pulling six-inch-thick cables of wires through holes atop the wall, while six other electricians work below them trying to pull the cables through a thick plastic cover. The foreman of the electricians' crew is clearly very nervous. Paul comments that he is an experienced electrician who has only recently been named foreman. His crew has been on the site since 2 a.m., struggling for seven hours now to get this cable installed. A carpentry crew that came to the site at 4 a.m. has been held up by these delays, and is starting to work around the electricians because another crew is scheduled to begin pouring cement for the wall in two hours. The carpentry foreman called to Paul as soon as he saw him, complaining loudly about the delays—delays mean overtime, overtime means higher costs, and higher costs can mean the jobs of the foreman and his crew, even if the delays were unavoidable. Paul tells the foreman that he will explain the delays in his report.

Paul sees the situation unfolding at the wall as potentially problematic, and he wants to avoid any mistakes that might create big expenses later. Paul approaches the nervous electrical foreman and asks him whether he thinks the twisted cable is a problem; the foreman recognizes the problem and fixes it. Later, Paul comments that, while many people have the technical knowledge to do this job, effective inspectors must plan ahead and do their homework to avoid problems and have the ability to maintain professional relationships and effective communications with others on the site.

As he moves out of the station, Paul gives a friendly wave to a crew of plumbers installing a pump in a narrow crawl space above the roof of the station. Once he climbs out of the station, he calls Rex on his walkie-talkie and tells him that the plumbing crew is installing the pump. Rex thanks him and tells him he will be right over to check the installation and to make certain there has been no damage to the rebar in the roof. Paul comments that, while each inspector works independently with different specialties and different assignments on the site, they are a team in the sense that "everyone watches out for each other." As Paul leaves the site, he walks over to a member of the traffic control crew and asks him to replace a stop sign across the street that had been graffitied over—not only is it a potential safety hazard, but it is an eyesore that may lead to complaints from neighborhood merchants.

Across town, another group of inspectors works in a very different setting, using very different techniques.  Here, the inspectors are involved in some of the last stages of the construction of the Orange Line, an elevated and surface rail line that will, when it opens in another six months, serve residents of the areas south and east of downtown Los Angeles.  The rail line is almost completely finished—tracks have been laid, staircases installed, electrical hookups completed.  Other than the three-person survey crew working its way along the length of the track, the only other workers at the site are installing electric fixtures, putting up signs, and finishing the painting of handrails and a few other features.  There is an unhurried, quiet feeling to the worksite.

The crew stand around the van, sipping coffee from steel thermos bottles.  The van is very much an "office on wheels" for the crew—it has room to seat four, with a small drafting table built from plywood and two-by-fours attached to one wall.  A plywood rack provides a place to hold blueprints and maps.  The back of the van is piled high with equipment and tool boxes that are needed in any job site.  The crew chief sits at the drafting table, reviewing plans for the station and filling in a series of elevation sheets that reveal the position the track is supposed to have according to specifications.  To determine these positions, the chief must use his "most important tool": a hand calculator that he has previously input with special programs that allow him to determine the proper placement of the rails to a one-eighth-inch tolerance, even when they have turns and subtle twists.  These twists, which the chief calls "spirals," mean the rails actually form a parabola, even though it may not be visible to the naked eye.  Without these spirals, the trains would not be able to negotiate turns safely.

The crew's job is to make certain the tracks are in exact placement according to plans.  This is the final quality control check and certification that the line was constructed properly.  The positions of the track are measured in relation to control points that have previously been set at a number of fixed, unchanging locations.  In addition to the spiraling of the rails, this site has an additional complication for the crew:  the rails sit on elevated platforms more than 40 feet high, requiring a series of calculations to move from three control points on the ground at the nearest traffic intersection over and up to the rail line.  The chief comments that these calculations force surveyors to develop an "algebraic mind" and the ability to place objects from two-dimensional maps and drawings into the three-dimensional world. While the chief works for 45 minutes on the next set of calculations, crew members begin unloading the equipment they will need for today's work.

Three elements make up the set of equipment used by a survey team. The main tool is an electronic distance measurement (EDM) machine, which the crew calls a "gun." Mounted on a tripod, the EDM contains sophisticated electronic systems and a laser, permitting immediate calculation of elevations and distances for objects that are "shot" by the operator. The gun must be placed in a precise location that has been carefully established in relation to the ground control points; measurements are made in relation to a "traverse line"—a straight line established between two control points that are in known locations. The second element in the survey equipment is the "back site"—a reflective prism sitting atop a tripod over the second point on the traverse line that provides the base from which any objects within the 500-foot range of the EDM machine can be precisely measured. Measurements are made using the third element in the survey system—a "linker rod" that is placed on each object that is to be measured and sighted through the EDM's viewfinder. The laser in the EDM bounces off the rod and back to the machine, where the electronic systems in the machine calculate the distance to the object. These measurements are compared against the figures calculated by the chief to determine if the objects (here, the rails) are in proper position. As noted above, a deviation of more than one-eighth inch will be considered outside of specifications and require the contractor to correct the deficiency.

As the crew moves to the elevated train station, each member of the team assumes his position. The chain man uses a plumb bob to set the back site directly above a "PK" nail that has been driven into the concrete rail bed at a carefully determined temporary control point. The instrument man does the same with the EDM machine, but is unable to correct the alignment between the machine and the back site without the help of the chief—he has been working as an instrument man for only three months and has not yet mastered many aspects of the operation of this complex machine. Once the instrument is in place, the chief calls to the chain man over the walkie-talkie, directing him to the first site to be measured. The chain man tries to predict where the chief might next send him, and must take only a few steps to find the proper placement.  He places the base of the linker rod on the marked spot, pulls a level from his tool belt, and uses it to ensure that the rod is directly perpendicular to the spot. The chain man comments that many of the tools in his belt are homemade—surveying is such a specialized field that it has become tradition that surveyors will make many tools that are not commercially available, just as they must often study on their own to learn how to operate new equipment or to solve problems they have never faced before.  When he calls "mark" over the radio, the instrument man tells the chief what the reading is.  The chief enters the reading and any variation from specifications in the elevation sheet.  When the chief is satisfied, he orders the chain man to move to the next spot, and the cycle repeats itself until the 500-foot section of track on both rail lines has been checked.

During a break later that afternoon, the chief begins to talk about the "global positioning system" (GPS)—a surveying system that uses a network of space-based satellites to fix on any object on the earth's surface.  GPS is not yet accurate enough to perform the kind of precision work the crew is doing on the Orange Line, but the chief believes it will eventually replace much of the technology currently in use in surveying.

In this chapter we have moved from a general characterization of the four firms in our sample to a more detailed description of the seven jobs we observed.  Next, in Chapter Four, we raise the power of magnification another notch to present our observations of the generic skills and work-related dispositions used by these workers on the job.

# SKILLS AT WORK

In this chapter, we show how several key skills and dispositions are applied in the context of the firms and jobs described in Chapter Two and the associated communities of practice. We examine four areas—problem solving, team work, communications, and work-related dispositions—in the seven jobs we studied. Examining them separately is necessary to understand how skills vary according to job, community of practice, and work setting. These distinctions are common in the research and policy literature (including our own previous research), and thus facilitate rough comparisons of findings across studies.

We find that the skills and dispositions that we observed are important, even central, to the performance of work in these jobs and settings and salient to the workers themselves. However, how these skills and dispositions are both applied and conceived vary as jobs and settings vary. As a result, the kinds of generic skills and work-related dispositions that many believe are necessary for new workplaces (outlined in Chapter Two) may reflect a true picture of generic skills at work, but the picture is not a simple one.

## PROBLEM SOLVING AT WORK

Our interviews and work observations enabled us to see how problems are defined in jobs, how workers apply skills to solve these problems, and how problem solving is construed by their community of practice. These problem-solving activities also illuminate other skill areas that we discuss later—team work, communications, and work-related dispositions.

## Quality Assurance and Quality Control

Construction inspectors view their work as "quality assurance," where they must achieve quality standards. Their job as inspectors is to determine whether the construction is being accomplished as required by the job specifications. Specifications are legal documents that can be used to guarantee that construction is completed precisely as contracted. The specifications both guide their inquiry during "in-process" inspection (i.e., signal what to look for in a particular situation) and represent the quality standard—how the construction must be done—during "back end" inspection. A typical inspection problem occurs when an inspector finds some discrepancy between the specifications and the construction and then must identify the source of the discrepancy and how to get the error corrected. (As discussed in a later section of this chapter, an inspector needs particular communication skills to deal with discrepancies in a manner that does not slow down the job or create tensions with the contractors.) The following example from our field notes illustrates a problem situation:

> A vice president of the contracting company and the lead inspector discuss a problem they must resolve: This morning a wall was poured before placing the rebar. [Rebar reinforces the wall, and reinforcement is particularly important in an underground subway station in an earthquake-prone area.] The inspector discussed the rebar with the foreman, but it was missed. When the inspector went back, they were completing the pour and he could see that the rebar was not in place. The lead inspector required that they replace the rebar. The vice president calls the design engineer on the speaker phone for advice on how to reduce disruption of other construction that is in compliance. They know they have to tear out the wall. They discuss alternatives, and decide to take the most conservative approach—chipping away the wall. The inspector asks for clarification on how the rework would be done so he can advise his inspectors. The lead inspector also gets a copy of the foreman's plans and notes, which show that the foreman discussed the placement in the notes but did not show it on the drawings. He tells the observer that this was a serious problem and that he will work to get that foreman off the job if he makes another mistake.

> Robert asks the electricians to stop working momentarily while he visually inspects that the conduit they have just placed is the correct

quality and size. The electricians continue and Robert returns to the office to check the plans for the electrical subcontractor. The foreman says his plans show conduits (in some areas), but Robert's plans do not. He checks to see if the plans have been changed or if changes are pending. Since they have not changed, he notifies the subcontractor's quality control chief to report the discrepancy. The quality control chief concurs that the subcontractor needs to comply, and promises to follow up with the foreman. Robert stops for a cup of coffee and a muffin while he writes notes. About fifteen minutes after Robert first inspected the conduit, he is ready to go back on site.

Quality control does not stop with construction, because damage of completed work is also a constant concern:

> The inspector and the contractor's quality control chief discuss damaged conduit openings. A crane rolled over several of the metal projections that emerge at the floor level. The conduits house various cables, and their installation was completed and signed off. Now the cement subcontractor may be required to pay for the repair. The inspector writes notes in his book and will write a damage report when he returns to his office. He consults plans (kept folded inside his safety vest) and writes specifications and numbers into his notes. He shows the damage to the concrete subcontractor, who nods his head "yes." No one is very upset. The subcontractor had laborers directing the crane, but the area is quite small, so the "accident" occurred.

Construction inspectors must also be vigilant about safety, to prevent accidents that then become problems. There are many hazards in subway construction, and inspectors are constantly checking for and correcting small hazards (e.g., standing water or inadequate lighting) and life-threatening dangers (e.g., temporarily constructed walkways and roadways that can loosen and fall on workmen below). Contractors facing tight schedules—such as restoring a street over the weekend before Monday morning rush hour—may focus on speed and pay less attention to safety.

The work of survey inspectors is similar to that of construction inspectors in that both perform back-end quality control functions (e.g., checking the elevation and horizontal placement of the train tracks, as discussed in Chapter Two). Survey inspectors also have a quality assurance function:  they measure precisely the proper location of various items of construction, and place stakes in the ground that guide and direct the construction.  If done properly by the survey crew and complied with by construction workers, the survey can prevent errors that are costly to contractors and can potentially threaten public safety.

Survey inspectors themselves define their work as problem solving: "the nature of surveying, though, is that there are constantly new problems to solve." And since the survey is a legal document, and inspectors are responsible for the correctness of their measurement, the crew takes its work very seriously.  Crew members describe their work as "exacting": there is no room for "guesswork."

In the following brief example, the crew is figuring out placement of manholes along a future trackway.

> The chief informs the crew that their task for the morning is to move through the last section of the job and set stakes for the height of each manhole.  The chief consults various sets of plans, looking for manholes.  Three different types of manholes are located on different sets of plans, which contain references to still other maps, drawings, and elevations in the packet.  Once the chief has identified all, he instructs the instrument man how to complete the elevation sheets.  This includes precise labeling of each manhole, the elevation, and the distance from the selected control point.  With the instrument man recording, the chief reads the name of the object and the location (referring to a scale on the base of the map).  The instrument man reads the numbers back, while the rod man listens attentively to catch any errors.  Once the manholes are located, the instrument man sets up the tripod and sights two vertical control points.  The chief directs the rod man to the first targeted manhole, which is measured using the linker rod.  The rod man labels the first stake with the proper height, and the chief drives it in.

Mapping from two-dimensional diagrams to the three-dimensional world is an important skill that surveyors must develop.  They talk about the need to have an "algebraic mind" that enables them to see the big picture and determine if the calculations and subsequent markings of specific objects in the field are logically consistent with the whole construction project.

The supervisor showed me a manhole cover that was placed in a sidewalk gutter rather than the middle of the street. In his view, the surveyor, builder, and contractor all failed to ask themselves whether the placement "made sense." If they had thought this through, they probably would have checked the plans and found a more proper placement.

Unlike any of the other jobs we studied, survey inspection requires mathematical problem solving. A large portion of the chief's job is calculating the exact horizontal and vertical placement of objects in the field from two-dimensional plan specifications. The calculations can be straightforward or complex, depending on the situation. According to the chief, surveyors' math skills are in demand at the worksite, and contractors will often ask them to make calculations. This gives surveyors a feeling of autonomy at the worksite—"kind of like being our own bosses." Other professionals also call on surveyors to help solve problems.

A civil engineer called on the radio to ask a question about a staircase at a particular station. The top of a staircase was going to fall one inch short of the platform, and the engineer needed help in understanding why so he could craft a solution. Over the radio, without performing calculations, the chief was able to understand the problem being described. He formulated a hypothesis and made some simple calculations to confirm it. The chief told the observer that he recognized the problem from the description and used calculations to justify his assertions to the engineer.

## Situation Assessment

The home health care worker is the "eyes and ears" of an extended patient care team, where each patient represents a "problem" that needs resolution. The aide or LVN deals with a particular patient's needs over the prescribed course of care through regular home visits. Depending on the patient, these visits generally occur once or twice a week for a nine-week period (although visits to diabetic patients can last six to nine months). We characterize their interactions with patients as "situation assessment" because, in addition to providing care, their role is to gather information about the patient's condition to report back to the case manager (usually a registered nurse) and to determine if the patient's condition warrants other than the currently prescribed action. Because each patient's situation is different—with respect to both medical and familial aspects—each case is unique. Thus, while the home health worker can follow standard protocols for gathering some information (e.g., patient weight, eating, sleeping, and medicating habits), she also has specific patient care tasks to carry out (e.g., bathing patients, changing bandages). She must also be on the lookout for any signs of physical abuse or deterioration, which she must report to the case manager.

Importantly, the home care worker must also assess and *interpret* the patient's current condition in the home care context. This home context provides clues for judging the information that the patient gives (or withholds) or for determining what aspects of the context assist or hamper the patient's care. Often patients are poor information sources because their illness affects their ability to think clearly or to report events accurately. Thus, the home care worker must get other information to help make an assessment and determine further action:

> The big concern was that the patient had pulled off one of his toe-nails for no apparent reason. They [the home care worker and a family member] scolded him like a young child and kept asking him why he did it. But his explanation was impossible to understand. They spent several minutes talking about it, trying to figure out why and when he did it.

In the course of their visits, LVNs must also diagnose problems they encounter and educate patients and household caregivers in ways that assist proper treatment.

> At this point, the wife said that sometimes her husband experiences tremors, but that on the bottle of his Ventolin [his asthma medicine], it lists tremors as a side effect. The aide asks about his dosage and if the tremors occur soon after he's taken the medicine. The response suggested that the Ventolin was not causing the tremors, and she made a note of the problem. She asked the wife whether they had told the doctor about these side effects. The wife responded that she had not. The aide advised her to discuss this with the neurologist at their next appointment.

## Troubleshooting Electronic Systems

Most of the time, equipment technicians at MPM and traffic signal technicians maintain and repair electronic equipment. The problem is defined as achieving desired equipment performance. When the equipment or system breaks down, the technicians must know how to troubleshoot—to identify the problem and fix it. When signal techs install new "beta" technology, the engineers who design the systems may not know how the equipment will perform in the field. Thus, techs must study wiring diagrams and work through problems to make the systems work.

The work context of each job places different constraints on troubleshooting. For traffic signal technicians, the pace of work is variable. It can be routine maintenance in the shop or field, or response to an emergency. Technicians face both routine and infrequent problem situations. They have to be familiar with various models of equipment (new electronic, cellular, or radar communications and older, simple electro-mechanical switches) and with various traffic management configurations (some of which include rail in addition to cars and pedestrians). Given these conditions, technicians feel that experience is the key to problem solving success:

> "You can't understand what it's like to troubleshoot a problem in the field until you are out there at two o'clock in the morning in the rain, and there's smoke coming out of the pull box. You can't teach that."

Although equipment technicians at MPM do not have to work in inclement weather, they work with very sensitive equipment in "clean room" conditions where, for example, a small electric shock can burn a hole in a chip that might affect the performance of a multi-million dollar satellite. Technicians describe their work as stressful and fast-paced because "down time is money."[1] Since the manufacturing technology is changing rapidly, new equipment is always arriving, and its floor life can be as short as six months.

---

[1] Recent growth, which produced a shortage of technicians in this area, also contributed to the stressful nature of the job.

As discussed in Chapter Three, in both jobs the organization attempts to manage the maintenance and troubleshooting activities. At MPM, technicians input information into the semiconductor productivity network (SPN), which monitors the condition of the equipment by indicating when a machine is down and by keeping a maintenance and repair history. The traffic surveillance system monitors traffic movements at major intersections and reports failures. But since this system monitors only some of the intersections, problems may be identified by the public or over the radio by public service workers (e.g., police, firefighters). Because these reports—particularly those from the public—can be incomplete or inaccurate, signal techs may have difficulty predicting the problem they will face. Experienced techs have most intersections memorized and, as soon as the call comes in, will begin to anticipate what might be wrong at a particular intersection and how to fix it.

Experienced technicians in both lines of work emphasize the need for a problem solving strategy in addition to any technical skills required for effective troubleshooting. One equipment technician described problem solving in the following way:

> "Your problem solving method—train of thoughts, the approach—is probably more important than their technical skill, what they know specifically. A lot of people know a lot about mechanics, chemistry, physics, and such, but when it comes to solving problems, they do not have the approach. Therefore, the knowledge they have is useless."

A signal technician supervisor described problem solving as "thinking in a logical sequence." And a technician noted that "troubleshooting procedures will save you a lot of time":

> While driving out to the field, the observer asked the tech how he proceeds at a flashing intersection. The technician explained that he tried to be systematic in troubleshooting. First, he will check the current at the hand hole nearest the controller cabinet, which will direct him to the cabinet or the field as the source of the problem. If it's in the field, he moves to the opposite corner and tests to determine if the problem is on one side of the intersection or the other. Finally, he will look for ant damage or other sources of wire damage.

Rex hooked a conflict monitor up to several machines on his desk and opened up a manual and diagram. He explained that it was a good monitor, and as he ran it through various tests he wrote numbers down on the diagram. He referred to this procedure as "mapping out" the good monitor. He then compared the "good" numbers with those obtained by running the damaged monitor through the same sequence of tests. Rex said he used this technique frequently.

As mentioned above, technicians believe that experience is crucial to problem solving success. Experience enables technicians to develop a mental model of the system that helps them solve problems: "You kind of have to know how one thing affects the system. That's a good thing for troubleshooting."

## Testing Components

Test technicians process batches of components that arrive with specific instructions about which tests must be conducted. Technicians must monitor the process of moving batches through the tests as well as performing the tests with the aid of various machines. As discussed below, these technicians manage the flow of work in their cell and are trained to operate all of the machines. When problems arise in this job and setting, they are typically associated with operating the test equipment. The following example describes how Henry, a new technician, solved a problem he faced.

Henry begins the testing by pulling out the plastic pouch containing the chips, the shop drawings, and some notes on the work that had been done thus far on the lot. He starts by counting the number of chips and, although two are missing, proceeds with the tests. He begins by pressing chips into the test board, but stops after three are mounted. He tells the observer that he is uncertain whether he has placed them in the proper orientation. He looks for Paul (acknowledged by the cell as the most expert technician), but he has walked away from the cell. Henry goes to the ovens to see if there is another board with similar chips in there, but there are none mounted. He returns to his work area and grabs the "fluke millimeter" tester and the chip design manual. He opens to the page for the chip in question, and lays one on the page in the same orientation as the diagram in the book. He uses the tester to connect between individual sockets on the test board, trying to figure out which cir-

cuits connect to each other. He compares the readouts on the tester
to the specifications in the manual until he has confirmed the
proper orientation of the chips. He then completes inserting the
chips in the board.

In this example, Henry figures out a way to solve his problem when
the most efficient solution—asking Paul for help—is not available. In
this community of practice, technicians are expected to face and
solve problems as a matter of routine. Like other technicians we
studied, they believe expertise develops with experience. And, while
all technicians can solve problems, "experienced people are expected
to see and predict problems." Furthermore, according to their supervisor, the performance standard for test cell technicians rests on
the team's problem solving capabilities, not on an individual's "units
per hour" (a productivity measurement widely used in other firms
and in other departments at MPM).

## TEAMWORK—MORE THAN "JUST GETTING ALONG"

In the workplaces we studied, conceptions of teamwork ran the
gamut from getting along with co-workers to specific relationships
and roles between individual workers that were necessary for accomplishing the task at hand. Not surprisingly, the ability to get
along with co-workers was valued in every job we examined. But
"just getting along" is clearly an insufficient description of teamwork
skills required for the work observed in this study. Rather, an effective team is comprised of members who have similar goals and standards for task completion.[2] As one traffic signal technician told us:

> "If it's a team I can put together, we do excellent work. If it's a team
> I'm thrown together with, it's difficult because it's a lot slower pro-
> cess. There are some people who work together really good and
> some people that don't—that don't necessarily agree on quality of

---

[2]Similarly, a recent study of unit cohesion in the military distinguished between social
cohesion (e.g., liking or getting along with others) and task cohesion, and concluded
the following: "It is not necessary to like someone to work with them, so long as
members share a commitment to the group's objectives" (*Sexual Orientation and U.S.
Military Personnel Policy: Options and Assessments*, RAND, MR-323-OSD, 1993, p.
330).

work and so forth. And it makes it difficult for me to do the type of work I want to do if they're not holding up their end."

We identified three overlapping aspects of team or group work that illustrate a variety of team arrangements and require different worker skills and behaviors (see Table 4.1).

## Self-Managing Teams

First, the traditional conception of self-managing work groups generally characterizes teamwork in two jobs: survey inspectors and test cell associates. As discussed in the overview of jobs in Chapter Three, a party chief heads the survey team, which consists of himself (who organizes work and makes complex calculations), an instru-

### Table 4.1

### Characteristics of Work Groups

| Job | Autonomous/ Self-Managing | Distributed Knowledge | Independent Work |
|---|---|---|---|
| Traffic signal technician | | | Shop work<br>Team for short-term problem solving (e.g., emergencies) |
| Home health aide/LVN | | Patient care team with many specialists<br>Distributed authority | Patient care in home |
| Test-cell associate | "Leaderless" team | | Independently perform tests |
| Equipment technician | | May specialize in particular machines | Independently repair and maintain machines |
| Survey inspector | Chief manages crew | Chief plus two instrument men | |
| Construction inspector | | Construction specialty | Independent inspection, but informal, "virtual" team (see text) |

ment man (who checks calculations), and a rod man (who moves equipment from point to point).

The Z1 Test Cell at MPM has four members who are cross-trained to perform all the tasks and operate all the equipment to complete final testing and quality certification on complex microprocessors. Each member of the cell works independently, running batches of chips through a sequence of tests. Managers describe the team as "leaderless" because it is unsupervised and requires team members to make decisions collectively to organize their own work. As discussed in the previous chapter, the team member with the most experience and education is often sought out to make decisions, train others, or help solve particular problems. The self-managing aspect of this team is evident in the following statement:

> "If it's an issue that deals with work within our cell, then we try and discuss it among ourselves. And then that's passed along to our supervisor."

## Distributed Knowledge

A second important characteristic of the work teams is the distribution of knowledge, skills, and sometimes authority among individuals. These teams can be formally recognized and supported by the organization, or informally constituted by team members themselves. The survey inspector team, for example, is composed of individuals of different rank and skill—with party chief as the acknowledged leader—and a survey expert who can perform all tasks and functions of the individual crew members. The crew members receive enough cross training to fill in for one another as needed, so that work can continue, albeit at a slower pace. The different roles are reinforced in the community of practice through union rules and regulations that designate both status and levels of skill or knowledge (e.g., journeyman or apprentice status).

At first glance, home health care providers and construction inspectors appear to be working independently to carry out specific jobs that align with their specialty. But home health providers are members of a large managed-care team, characterized by both distributed knowledge and authority linked to special certification. Knowledge is distributed among the various specialists that are part of the team—aides, doctors, nurses, physical or speech therapists, pharmacists, and so on. Similarly, different specialists or professionals have different levels of authority in the team related to their certification. Aides and LVNs, for example, are not permitted to perform several tasks in the nurses' domain, including initial patient assessment, plan of care, evaluation, and deciding whether or not a patient needs to continue with care. An agency supervisor acknowledges that not all of the home care staff have learned how to perform effectively in teams, but they continue to "push them toward that with some of the accountability."

Because of liability issues associated with health care and certification policies, the authority structure is formalized through work rules and procedures. As discussed below, for example, the aide must communicate with other health care professionals about events and issues that lie outside her own authority, and she must complete paperwork that contributes to a written record of each patient's case.

Construction inspectors perform their jobs as members of a "virtual" team which, in their minds, helps improve the quality and efficiency of the work. These inspectors have specialized knowledge (e.g., in concrete work, electrical work) that defines their individual inspection tasks; some are specialists in several disciplines. While each inspector makes rounds to inspect areas specifically related to his discipline, he is on the alert for activity in the other disciplines. When he spots a problem or potential problem or knows that the work has reached an inspection point, he contacts the appropriate inspector by radio. The virtual team is not a formal entity in the organization, but the creation of this community of practice in support of their high-quality work standards.

## Independent Work

Finally, traffic signal technicians and test technicians (MPM) work independently, for the most part. Traffic signal technicians work independently in the shop: "a lot of what we do as techs, we do alone."[3] Work assignments by the supervisor are flexible: techs are generally assigned to zones that include approximately 110–130 intersections. Two techs work in the electronics shop, two assistant techs work in the "head" shop, and a three- to four-man construction crew is responsible for major knockdowns, new construction, and other major repairs. Field teams may form for short-term problem solving or specific activities—replacement of a control cabinet in the field, for example, is a two-person job. Traffic signal techs also team with others to respond to emergency situations. This teamwork is problem-focused and short-term.

As the following example illustrates, traffic signal technicians' work tends to be less specialized than work on other jobs. Whereas some technicians may spend more time in the shop because they prefer shop work and are good at troubleshooting repairs, as a group the technicians possess similar knowledge and skills, with some more expert than others. Expertise—or what the technicians call "common sense"—is usually equated with experience.

> "Recently I had a problem when it was raining and we had all kinds of [warning] lights going on and simultaneously there were things that weren't supposed to be going on. I'd gotten down to the cabinet and I couldn't figure out what was going on in the cabinet, and I asked for somebody to come out there and give me a hand with it. Together, we spent another two to three hours trying to figure out what was going on. I often ask for people with a little more experience to come out and help. It's usually an emergency type condition that you need to ask for help."

The technicians' community of practice supports sharing of expertise when there is a problem to solve. If the problem is one that techs have not encountered before, they will come together as a group to diagnose the situation. They also regularly meet to "talk about what's going on." As we discuss further in Chapter Five, a community of practice that supports learning and sharing of expertise among its members is a vital source of training, particularly in firms that have few resources for formal training.

---

[3]In the shop, technicians have discretion over their day-to-day work. One tech, for example, "saves up" until he gets several items of the same type (e.g., conflict monitors). He works on these for a week or two, then switches to the next item.

As described earlier, equipment technicians at MPM are responsible for repair and maintenance of sophisticated machines used to develop new microprocessor manufacturing technology. Work across shifts is coordinated through daily transition meetings, where technicians discuss which machines are down and what needs to be done. Techs work independently, first checking the semiconductor productivity network, and then performing various tasks. Techs also specialize in repair of particular machines that they know well. One particularly expensive and complicated machine at MPM has a designated technician assigned to watch over its operation.

Teaming to solve repair problems is temporary, flexible, and ad hoc. When a tech is having trouble with a machine, it's considered acceptable to leave the repair for someone on a later shift who is more expert at repairing that particular piece of equipment. A tech may also seek assistance from techs in other departments to troubleshoot repairs. If the techs repeatedly fail to make a repair, they notify their manager.

The repair work is independent, but operators will converse with technicians and call on them for help when a machine malfunctions. Like the traffic signal technicians, the equipment technicians in the group possess similar skills, with some specialization. Knowledge is distributed not by specialty—as in home health and construction or survey inspection—but by virtue of a technician's experience, which presumably gives him broader and deeper knowledge and skills than the newcomer.

## DISPOSITIONS AND ATTITUDES AT WORK

As discussed in Chapter Two, there is little empirical research on dispositions, attitudes, or other "noncognitive" aspects of work behavior from sociocultural or other perspectives. We attempted to describe dispositions from our observations of workers and management in various worksites and then define themes that appear to cut across them.[4] This is a tentative step toward taking the social context

---

[4]The interviews prompted all respondents to discuss skills needed in the target jobs. In addition, as part of the cognitive task analysis, we asked frontline workers to discuss the attitudes and dispositions at work that served individuals well or poorly.

of work into account, rather than simply declaring that worker "attitudes" are important.

Study participants were unanimous in believing that dispositions were critical to success.  They frequently mentioned dispositions, as defined in Chapter Two (e.g., conscientious, self-directed, persistent, hard-working).  Some respondents discussed feelings and interpersonal relationships, such as a sense of closeness or mutual respect, as being important qualities.  We decided to incorporate these characteristics into our analysis as well.  We identified and compared dispositions along three somewhat overlapping themes: task/organization, community of practice, and quality standards (see Table 4.2).  Task/organization refers to dispositions related primarily to formal job characteristics, such as having to work in teams or accept supervision.  This contrasts with dispositions that the community of practice defines as important, irrespective of the work organization or management's views.  Finally, workers often discussed dispositions in relation to quality performance standards, as defined by the firm, norms of practice, or individual workers.

### Inspectors

The survey crew discussed personal characteristics for their work across all three themes.  First, because the task requires teamwork, they emphasized cooperation and the need to work together.  But the survey crew also expressed a closeness and interdependence that other teams did not.  They described their team as an "intimate situation," in which the members must rely on one another in an atmosphere of "mutual respect."  One crew member discussed this in relation to a change in surveying practice:

> "It's changed.  In the old days it was a party chief, and he'd scream at the apprentices, and how it's just done the way it's done.  Like [an] in-the-Army type thing.  And today it's a lot more sophisticated, and it's more of a team and a mutual respect."

The party chief echoed this sense of interdependence and thus the need for a collaborative and cooperative attitude: "you want a crew that will back you up.  You don't want somebody . . . trying to trip you up."

Table 4.2

**Dispositions and Other Characteristics**

| Job | Task/Organization | Practice | Quality Standard |
|---|---|---|---|
| Survey inspector | Love a challenge<br>Attention<br>Cooperate<br>Anticipate problems | Mutual respect<br>Reliance<br>Confidence<br>Prepared to work | Professional standards<br>Assume liability |
| Construction inspector | Manage people<br>Plan ahead<br>Deal with confrontation<br>Independent | Know and do your own job<br>Ask for help | Conscientious<br>Vigilant<br>Assume liability<br>Integrity |
| Home health provider | Independent<br>Tolerant of oversight<br>Accept flexible scheduling | Friendliness<br>"Bedside manners"<br>Patience | Individual standard<br>Professional standard<br>Personal liability |
| Test cell technician | Flexible<br>Willingness to do repetitive work<br>Teamwork<br>Willing to learn | | Accurate and thorough |
| Equipment technician | Independent<br>Handle pressure<br>"Man over machine"<br>Flexible | | Individual performance<br>Affects productivity |
| Traffic signal technician | Self-motivated<br>Tolerant of variable pace | Don't pass problems off<br>Don't slack off | Individual standard<br>Assume liability |

Surveyors also identified several dispositions as crucial to success: "love a challenge," attention to detail, anticipate problems before they arise. As the head of the crew, the party chief also needs "interpersonal relations skills to handle the crew" and interactions with contractors on the job site.

Surveyors' emphasis on quality work, however, derives not so much from a desire to do a good job for the company (as with the equipment technicians at MPM) or to meet an individual standard (as with home health aides and LVNs), but from their professional standards as surveyors.  Their sense of professionalism and professional standards sets up expectations that good surveyors, by definition, have a "go-for-it" attitude and will show extra effort by, for example, taking plans home to prepare for the next day's work or making calculations several ways to double-check their accuracy.  A surveyor should have "confidence in his professionalism" and, at the same time, "always second-guess [himself]."  If a decision or calculation is challenged, the surveyor should "assume he's wrong and go back and check it." And if he made a mistake, he must be "willing to take the heat."  The conscientious emphasis on quality complements the fact that the survey is a legal document and the chief—and by extension the crew—is liable for its accuracy.

Construction inspectors also face liability issues and have concerns about quality that require them to have a conscientious attitude toward their work (i.e., have discipline necessary to read and understand and verify) and to be prepared to anticipate each inspection task—"he is one step ahead of the contractor instead of behind him":

> At the closing of the wall, the "pace of the jobs seems to accelerate."
> As electricians make installations, carpenters follow as closely as possible to close things up.  "I have to keep ahead of the carpenters and inspect the electrical work.  Meantime, I have to watch the carpenters, who may take safety chances.  I have to ensure that everything that has been installed has been inspected and re-inspected before that cement wall goes in."

The inspector's quality assurance role is sometimes in conflict with the contractors and subcontractors, whose incentives are to build in accordance with contract requirements and to make a profit doing so.  Much of the construction inspectors' discussion of dispositions hinges on this tension.  When problems arise, the inspector often needs negotiation skills (discussed below in the section on communications) and must "be able to deal with confrontation."  To keep the job running smoothly, it is important that the inspector not "take personal feelings [about the contractor] into a work problem," but "learn how to present an issue without personal involvement."  Even in the absence of problems, inspectors cite the need for interpersonal skills to communicate with people at different educational levels (from high school graduates to Ph.D.s) and different specialties.

Although construction inspectors do not use the term "profession" to describe their standard of practice, they define codes of behavior that are acceptable or unacceptable. As described above, a good inspector recognizes his quality assurance role and all that it entails. He is someone whose disposition is to "move around and do his inspections. He's not standing around with the foreman telling jokes and stories." Instead, the construction inspector feels obliged to know and understand the general plan, not just those associated with his specialty. Armed with this knowledge and disposition to be self-directed, the "team" of inspectors constantly alert each other of construction activities warranting each specialist's attention. At the same time, expert inspectors look down on others who, in their eyes, attempt to go beyond the boundaries of the job. Instead of inspecting according to the plans or asking for assistance interpreting the plans, they attempt to "redesign the work" by questioning what the engineers specified. This diverts attention from getting the job done.

## Home Health Providers

Home health providers emphasized dispositions that reflect the organization of their work and the norms of the nursing profession. Because they spend most of their time visiting patients at home, they must be independent, hence self-directed, in their work habits. They must also be flexible, because their assignments and schedule can change quickly, and because each patient's particular needs determine how long each visit will take. Although home care providers must want to work independently, they must also be tolerant of oversight. The case manager has the authority to change visit schedules or even to direct providers to make visits outside their regular geographic area.

> "You are the low man on the totem pole, so you have to follow. You're getting orders from everybody. You have to have that type of attitude. If you don't . . . you have to find another job."

This oversight appears to be a distinguishing factor of home care work. As one aide told us: "many colleagues don't like home health because they feel someone is looking over their shoulder." She also felt that some supervisory staff "are hard on you" and would advise a new employee to "cover your behind at all times, because this is the type of job that you can get dinged."

Home care providers stress interpersonal relations in their dealings with patients.  Home care workers must be patient and friendly on the job and have good "bedside manners."  Patients appreciate these characteristics:

> I asked her generally about the services Sally (the LVN) provides, and the patient is very positive on Sally's work.  She emphasizes the word "temperament," indicating that staff in senior centers often have negative attitudes, don't smile, provide snappy answers, and spend a lot of time telling patients about their problems.  "Sick people don't need to hear about other peoples' problems."

Having bedside manners is more than being friendly and smiling, however.  Home care providers stress the need to be sensitive to patients' concerns as "she is a visitor in the patient's home and does not want to intrude or otherwise upset them."  While some patients do not want the provider out of their sight when in the home, others do not mind if she moves about freely.

Another aspect of bedside manners is providing care to people from different cultures and socioeconomic conditions.  To be culturally sensitive, the home care provider must be able to adjust her practice to accommodate differences and show respect for the patient's needs.

Home care workers may also have to deal with prejudice toward their own racial or ethnic group.  Agency policy permits a home care worker who confronts racial prejudice to refuse to provide service to that patient, but aides reported having resolved such situations on their own.

When home care providers discuss dispositions or feelings related to providing quality service, they emphasize individual standards as caregivers, not the broader "quality care" goals espoused by the health agency.  Quality can be linked to a personal sense of pride or mastery—for example, if a provider chooses to work with patients who display prejudice toward her rather than be reassigned.  Providing quality care requires the caregiver to "stay focused" and subordinate one's own feelings to serve the patient.  One African-

American provider expressed a preference for working with African-American patients because she feels competent in her knowledge of the culture and language and "understands where they're coming from." This connection, in her view, enables her to provide better-quality care.

## Test Cell and Equipment Technicians

Technicians at MPM did not discuss dispositions in terms of professional practice, but as requirements of the job. Both emphasized the need to be flexible and adaptable to change—organizational change for test cell associates and technology change for both. Interestingly, although the technicians characterized their work as variable and requiring one to "always learn new things," a human resources manager thought the jobs required "willingness to do repetitive work."

For test cell technicians, the most important dispositions are to work as part of the team, to be flexible in work assignments—on different machines, on different shifts, and sometimes on Saturdays—and to be "eager and willing to learn." Independence is less valued than teamwork because techs believe "two heads are better than one" in working through problems.

Test cell technicians and their supervisor discussed dispositions associated with quality in general terms. The supervisor, for example, discussed the need for some workers to develop a better "work ethic," which he defined as "care about the quality of their work."

Equipment technicians mentioned the need to deal with a high-stress environment and thought a "man over machine" attitude was important:

> "I think you've got to kind of be a little cocky, that you're not gonna let some stupid machine beat you. A machine might have a computer-guided something—it might be a laser, it might be robotic—but it's still a machine. And it can't do anything unless I'm there. And it's gonna do what I tell it to do."

Similarly, techs thought it was important to be open-minded about the possible source of problems: "It's not always an electronic problem, but sometimes mechanical."

Equipment technicians in this department at MPM often discussed their work in terms of its effect on productivity. An attitude that recognizes the link between equipment maintenance and production is important: you need to "maximize the up time" and "keep production running."

## Traffic Signal Technicians

Questions about work dispositions revealed some tensions in the traffic signal technician community. Technicians discussed the need to be tolerant of the variable pace of the job, where a normal slow pace is punctuated by emergency calls. Sometimes it's busy and sometimes not, so one periodically has "time on your hands" and must "deal with the ups and downs of the work flow." This requires technicians to be resourceful in finding work during down times. The job design requires that technicians work independently—they have shop work and a certain number of signals to maintain. Because their supervisors are often busy with other projects and have little time for oversight, they must be self-directed.

Technicians openly discuss how this work situation—little supervision and "time on your hands"—has developed a wide distribution of work dispositions: "We've got people from one extreme to the other and they're still getting by." As one tech explained:

> "It's a self-motivated thing here. You're either productive or you're not, and it depends on you 100 percent. They do not have a system of forced work. They have a maintenance procedure . . . but no system for making sure that it is done. So if a person is a reliable, self-motivated individual, he'll . . . accomplish that as best he can. The other people don't, aren't motivated, will do the minimum that they can get away with."

The techs talk about the "A team" and the "B team"—a tech's attitude toward the work determines to which he belongs. The community of practice is bifurcated: techs on the "A team" speak with frustration about techs who "skate through and get away with it" because management tolerates their behavior and because "other people here are conscientious enough to do the job properly." If a tech "slacks off" and doesn't do maintenance or try to figure out a problem situation he encounters, then other techs end up having to deal with those problems later on. This can happen when emergencies arise, or when techs who are on top of their own assigned signals must work overtime to correct problems that other less-conscientious techs have ignored. For the "A team" techs, it is unacceptable to "not do a proper repair and leave it for the next guy."

The variation in dispositions of individuals can affect the whole department. If too much overtime is clocked—in part to make up for less conscientious technicians—then the department can be questioned or criticized by higher management about exceeding their budget. Experienced technicians become demoralized—they love the work but hate the job. When asked how he would describe the job to a new employee, one tech was of two minds:

> The "work is neat. We have a long way to go as far as building morale in our particular department and making a work environment that you feel real comfortable about coming in . . ."

From the views of respondents in all three transportation management agencies, we can conclude that the traffic signal technician profession depends on motivated individuals who are willing to keep up with technology changes, including taking outside classes on their own time if necessary. Since specific courses or programs for training signal techs are rare, agencies and techs depend on on-the-job training to get beyond the basic skills and to learn to apply electronics knowledge to traffic signal work. Thus, it is particularly important for the community of practice to have healthy relationships—experienced technicians must work with newcomers to pass on their knowledge and skill and the working environment must support that relationship.

Finally, with respect to quality, techs view the lack of standards as a problem that creates different dispositions toward work and toward achieving quality standards.

> "Some guys don't do anything unless they get a call. They're not doing their maintenance. I have a higher standard than they [management] have."

The techs' supervisors mentioned some dispositions that they looked for which were not mentioned by technicians themselves. While both thought a willingness to learn was important, supervisors wanted techs who were motivated to take classes on their own time. Techs, on the other hand, tended to discuss opportunities to learn on-the-job (e.g., finding an expert tech to work with and learn from) and were critical of colleagues who "don't want to get updated." (As we discuss in the next chapter, some techs complained that management would not give them the time off to take courses they wanted to take.) Managers also want "flexible" techs who are willing to work in the field and in the shop: "We find a lot of guys who are well-educated don't care to go out and do that kind of [field] work."

## COMMUNICATION SKILLS

As we indicated in Chapter Two, we examined the application of communication skills along four traditional axes: *audience* (who is communicated with); *purpose* (why they are communicated with); *style* (the way in which the communicator presents himself or herself); and *mode* (the means by which the communication is accomplished). Table 4.3 summarizes our findings.

### Audience

The workers we studied needed to be able to communicate effectively with audiences that differed on several major dimensions. An important distinction for frontline workers was internal versus external audiences—members of their own firms versus members of the public, including their firm's customers. Communication with patients and their families was a central part of the job of home health providers. Traffic signal engineers working in the field often had to communicate with motorists, the "customers" of the traffic signal system, who were not always in the best of moods; they also were called upon infrequently to provide testimony in court during suits in which the maintenance of intersections became an issue. Indeed, the primary audience for the engineers' maintenance logs was not their supervisors, but members of the legal profession involved in litigation with the city. This accounted for the strong emphasis, second only to the emphasis on safety itself, on accurate recordkeeping.

**Table 4.3**

**Communications Activities by Job**

| Job | Audience | Purpose | Style | Mode |
|---|---|---|---|---|
| Home health aides | Patients and family members<br>Other health care professionals | Elicit and provide information<br>Provide instructions | Amicable professional demeanor | Face-to-face conversation<br>Telephonic conversation<br>Written records |
| Traffic signal engineers | Other traffic signal engineers<br>Workers in other departments<br>Motorists<br>Courtroom participants<br>Supervisors | Provide information<br>Provide instructions<br>Request assistance | Amicable yet professional demeanor with public<br>Fluent English important | Face-to-face conversation<br>Radio transmission<br>Testimony<br>Written records and forms |
| Construction inspectors | Other inspectors<br>Contractors and construction workers | Provide information<br>Provide instructions<br>Negotiate | Amicable yet professional demeanor<br>Bilingual Spanish/English useful | Face-to-face conversation<br>Written reports |

**Table 4.3—continued**

| Job | Audience | Purpose | Style | Mode |
|---|---|---|---|---|
| Survey inspectors | Other survey crew members Construction workers | Provide information Provide instructions | Collegial manner | Face-to-face conversation Meetings Radio transmission |
| Test cell finish associates | Other test cell members Selected workers in other units | Provide information Schedule tests Provide assistance with procedures | English speaking less important because cells are grouped by primary language of most members | Face-to-face conversation Tracking sheets |
| Equipment technicians | Other test technicians Operators of machinery | Solve problems collectively Provide instructions on how to use machines | | Face-to-face conversation Operating instructions Written logs (hard copy and on-line) |

With the possible exception of home health aides, most workers communicated chiefly with internal audiences—members of their work group, co-workers, and supervisors. Construction and survey inspectors, for instance, communicated regularly with other inspectors as well as with contractors. Home health providers communicated with a variety of health professionals involved with the same patients, particularly nurses and social workers.

Finally, the workers in our study communicated with single individuals or small groups; their responsibilities did not include communicating to large groups (for example, leading meetings or giving presentations).

## Purpose

In both speech and writing, the most common purpose for communications skills was to convey an appropriate fact accurately. Home health providers report on the status of patient functioning and log their own activities, including facts such as mileage driven. Traffic signal technicians call in to order parts and maintain scrupulous maintenance records that may be subpoenaed. Construction inspectors communicate requirements, deficiencies, and approvals. Survey inspectors call out measurements.

The second most common purpose was to convey procedural information—instructions. Home health providers instruct patients and their family members. Construction inspectors tell contractors how to meet specifications and gain approvals. Equipment technicians write instructions for machine operators to lessen their maintenance burden.

In these communications of fact and procedure, accuracy is the most valued quality. Speed is also valued: time is money. Clarity is highly valued, including fluent pronunciation and legible writing, because lack of clarity hurts both accuracy and speed. The following quotation from a traffic signal engineer evidences the value he places on accuracy, brevity (i.e., speed), and clarity:

> We have radio communication. We have to be able to briefly explain what we want. [Say] I need an "eight-inch head and a round

vac JVC box with a center hole." That's something that comes up, and you have to explain what you want . . . and you have to understand what they're saying, too.

## Style

We observed that an amicable but professional demeanor was highly valued in all spoken communications. Such a demeanor was perceived to contribute to both the speed and quality of the communications by improving the ability and willingness of the listener to engage in communication. This was particularly important on jobs that required the worker to communicate directly with the public—such as the home health workers and, to a lesser extent, the traffic signal technicians. These audiences often included individuals who were hostile or uncommunicative for other reasons, perhaps in part because they were not themselves in a work context. A friendly self-presentation was also particularly valued in the work of construction inspectors, who frequently needed to negotiate with contractors to ensure that work proceeded as planned and per specifications. As one inspector told us, "it's basically a matter of communication, how you need to talk to the contractor and subcontractors . . . I think that the most important part of our job is to communicate." Without effective negotiation skills, inspectors risk violating the public trust in two ways; either by approving construction that is sloppy or does not meet specifications, or by creating conflict with the construction teams that may contribute to errors.

## Mode

Although all these workers had jobs in fields that had been recently infused with technological advances, neither their spoken nor written communications showed much reliance on advanced technology. Oral communication was accomplished primarily in person and secondarily by phone; most written communication was written by hand (even if it were eventually to be entered on-line by others). Forms were the most common technological adjunct to written communication on the job. All of these jobs required recordkeeping using forms.

Only the test cell associates and equipment technicians at MPM were observed to keep records on a computer (also using forms). Others—health agency and transportation construction—anticipate implementing electronic forms in the future.

In this chapter we have offered a detailed description and analysis of four areas of generic skills and work-related dispositions that are used on the job by the workers whom we observed. We have shown that these skills and dispositions figure prominently in the accomplishment of their work and that workers recognize the important contribution that such skills make to their performance. We have also demonstrated that, though generic in some senses, these skills nevertheless are used in quite specific ways on each job; accordingly, requirements for each can vary widely from one job to another. Finally, we have demonstrated that these skills, though sometimes distinguishable in theory, are in practice typically found together, suggesting that their contribution to the effective performance of work should be understood synergistically.

# Chapter Five

# ACQUIRING AND DEVELOPING WORKFORCE SKILLS

In Chapter Four, we described problem solving, teamwork, communication skills, and dispositions in technical work and discussed how their definition varies by work context. According to employers and workers, these general skills and dispositions are essential for effective job performance.

In this chapter, we discuss how employers perceive their changing skill demands and how their human resource policies, including recruitment, hiring, training, and compensation, support skill acquisition and development. We also examine the sensitivity of these policies to worker needs and the social organization of work.

We discuss the institutional context of worksites in turn along several common themes—conditions affecting skill needs, selection and hiring practices, and training, including formal training and opportunities to learn on the job. The data presented here (summarized in Table 5.1) lead to four major findings: Employers do not always understand the specific skill requirements of their frontline workforce, and their selection and hiring policies do not always enable them to acquire the skills they need. Employers do little to foster skill development among nonmanagerial workers, and in some instances they take courses of action that actually undermine skill development. Employers have few connections with educational institutions that might support skill development in their frontline workforce.

Table 5.1

**Skill Acquisition and Development**

| Firm | Conditions Affecting Skill Needs | Selection and Hiring | Training |
|---|---|---|---|
| MPM | Global market<br>Reorganized to flexible work teams<br>Rapid technology turnover<br>TQM companywide | No unions<br>90-day probationary period<br>Adequate supply in labor market<br>Career path linked to skills, wages | Integrated with business strategy<br>In-house cross-training<br>Planned OJT<br>Vendor training<br>Dedicated trainers |
| Health agency | TQM/CQI<br>Growth in home care<br>Managed care teams<br>Outsourcing strategy | Union contract and company policy affect hiring, wages, and promotion<br>Licensure | Industry tradition for continuous training to upgrade and recertify skills<br>Dedicated trainers<br>Planned OJT<br>Tuition reimbursement |
| Traffic management | Significant technology changes<br>Austerity<br>Short-staffed | Adequate supply in labor market<br>Civil service restrictions<br>Certification not required | No budget for training<br>OJT/job rotation<br>Community of practice trains<br>Tuition reimbursement |
| Transportation construction | TQM in some departments<br>Merger and downsizing | Adequate supply in labor market<br>Union involvement in hiring, wages<br>Certification encouraged | Training low priority in TA<br>Contractor supports training for certification<br>Union training for survey inspection<br>OJT integral to survey work |

# MICROPROCESSOR MANUFACTURING

At MPM, several factors contribute to the company's approach to securing the technological workforce it needs (see Table 5.1). First,

MPM competes globally to sell its product—its competitors are large companies in the United States, Germany, and Japan. As competitors in the global market, MPM operates plants in the United States and overseas, and distributes its development, production, and related activities among the plants to competitive advantage. The main activities of the plant we visited differ from other plants and affect the technical workforce they need locally. Whereas cheaper labor costs have sent many of the lower-skilled manufacturing jobs to the firm's overseas operations, the number of technical jobs has increased with this plant's emphasis on product development and manufacture of high-end components (such as those produced under contract for the military). Workers require higher technical skills to operate and maintain the high-tech equipment used in these activities.

A second, related factor is MPM's adoption of total quality management (TQM) practices to increase their ability to successfully compete. This transition, which began a few years ago and is still in process, has, in many respects, changed the organization and the way it does business. For the work groups that we studied, TQM completely transformed work processes for test cell associates, but has had little impact thus far on the work of equipment technicians, who are most affected by rapid changes in manufacturing technology.

An executive at MPM believes that these changes have increased skill needs in the jobs under study. By and large, managers at MPM report that they are able to hire skilled workers in the local labor market, then train them to work as test cell associates and equipment technicians. As we discuss in more detail in a following section, MPM is highly committed to training at all levels of the organization—training is an essential element in its business strategy.

## Selection and Hiring

The workforce at MPM is not unionized. When job openings occur, the company generally advertises through newspaper ads or by word of mouth. There is some limited contact with local technical schools—one test cell associate in our study was interviewed and hired after the technical school he graduated from sent his resume to

MPM.  Many jobs are filled through the bank of applications submitted by job seekers.

In hiring prospective employees, MPM first looks for previous technical experience in the field.  Interviews with supervisors—and sometimes team members—can make or break an applicant's chances.  The interview helps assess an applicant's English-speaking ability and what a trainer describes as "intangible qualities," such as the ability to ask questions and work as part of a team.[1]

While the human resources department has responsibility for setting educational requirements and salaries and for job market analysis, supervisors in each department make hiring decisions.  Once hired, technicians enter a 90-day probationary period.  Staff that don't work out are simply replaced.  To the human resources manager, the low "failure rate" indicates that MPM can get the skills it needs in the local direct labor market.  Others we spoke with at MPM generally agree, although an equipment technician felt that the high cost of living in the Los Angeles area depressed the availability of highly skilled technicians.  A trainer, however, expressed concern that many applicants seem overqualified because jobs in the area are in short supply.  He worries that MPM can lose its training investment if the economy improves and these workers leave after a few years.

## Training in MPM

At MPM, training is connected to the firm's strategic plan and reflects its recent adoption of TQM principles, as well as specific needs related to the products it makes and its customers.  An executive in one department we studied described his operations as "a witnessed area," where training is required by military standards and specifications, and for ISO 9000 international manufacturing specifications.[2]

---

[1]MPM management stresses teamwork for employees at all levels, whether or not they are members of formal teams, like the test cell associates.  Being a "team player" is valued in their TQM environment because each employee is expected to apply his or her specialty to solving problems and improving work processes for the common good.  A manager says they discourage "Lone Rangers" and "heroes" with a "let me show you how smart I am" attitude.

[2]ISO 9000 is a system of quality management standards that has become virtually required for firms to compete in many international markets.

Prior to the firm's adopting TQM a few years ago, a new employee was placed in the easiest job until the next employee was hired and then moved up the chain. Management accepted the fact that new employees receiving this on-the-job training reduced overall production output for some time. With TQM and the reorganization of some jobs into teams, MPM switched to a cross-training program in which progress is measured and each employee is certified to do all jobs. An executive explained that manufacturing has a "capacity-driven need [for skills]—not a demand for particular skills, but for flexibility." Cross-training provides this flexibility. Similarly, a human resources manager described cross-training as a strategy "not just for skill shortages, but for more effective operations." The firm "hires temps to fill short-term demands." The basic strategy was described as "grow our own": to produce the skills it needs in its own training program. While cross-training beyond the group level is a goal, it will be done "only if it makes sense, without forcing it."

While the commitment to training is strong in the firm, training delivery can vary by plant and subplant. It can be the responsibility of dedicated trainers in some areas (e.g., TQM for management) or subplants, or of supervisors or lead operators in others. MPM has recently formed a North America Training Team to develop companywide training standards for all the U.S. plants but, at the time of our study, training for the two jobs we studied differed somewhat. The corporate mission drives many training decisions, but the organization is still in transition to TQM, and thus some training practices or policies do not yet mesh with the overall vision.

## Test Cell Associates

Training for test/finish cell associates is organized around the concept of "subplant development," in which the subplant takes responsibility for training and has a dedicated trainer. Although the trainer does not have a specific budget for training purposes—he fills out a purchase order whenever he needs something—his requests have rarely been denied. The subplant analyzed previous training practices, which were driven largely by operators' requests. They found that while extensive time was spent training to "wire bond," few had problems with it (except for occasionally using the wrong wire). Rather, "non-operational" processes, as opposed to machine-related operations, appeared to cause more production problems. The subplant manager is putting together a series of non-operational training modules as part of the operators' career path, thus providing an incentive for workers to invest in training.  As the manager explained:

> "We are committed that these [the training modules] are going to be available; otherwise we are standing in the way of investment, which is not right."

Once the modules are completed, the supervisors will be responsible for carrying out the training program.  One supervisor has formed a team of representatives from different cells to create a new format for some of the technical manuals, which he described as engineering-oriented and not user-friendly.  The new formats will be incorporated into the training modules.  This participatory approach enhances employee involvement in the training process.  The firm considers employee input as necessary for success because "their view of what they need is better than management's view."

Planned on-the-job training to achieve cross-training consists of both classroom training and individual, one-on-one training in equal measure; some instruction is available on videotape. An "operations skills list" designates skills at three levels—0 for untrained, 1 for partially trained, 2 for fully skilled—and indicates training available for each, including how on-the-job training is linked with classroom training.  Each associate and the entire cell try to increase their scores, which relate to placement on the career path. As the associates acquire training to move up the career path, their wages increase with each step (e.g., associate #1 makes $6.25–$9.00 an hour; associate #3 makes $13–$14.50 an hour).  Performance evaluations using checklists have replaced written tests for skill certification because the trainer found that workers were "scared" by tests.  Productivity standards are relaxed while changes in training take place, but a higher quality standard is set.

During our observation periods, we noted that some instances of on-the-job training went well, while others revealed problems.  One trainee and an experienced technician visited another area so the trainee could learn to operate a particular machine that was about to be moved into the cell.  The operator who conducted the training appeared unsure; she repeatedly forgot and retraced steps, and failed to answer some of the trainee's questions. She had a difficult time explaining the paperwork for recording the test results. Although the trainee did not appear to have much difficulty when left to test some chips on his own, the experienced technician consulted the manual to double-check the paperwork requirements and discovered that the operator was following an erroneous procedure.

## Equipment Technicians

The technicians who repair and maintain the equipment in the wafer fabrication department have a more traditional on-the-job training program, which is part of their improvement strategy. New technicians receive no formal training when they start, but are instructed on the job by an expert technician. This trainer uses a combination of lecturing, coaching, and hands-on demonstration to bring new technicians up to speed. The technicians also receive training off-site, from equipment vendors or from personnel at another plant. If the technicians are having severe problems with the equipment and down time is high, the supervisor may send one or two technicians to classes to enhance their knowledge of the technology. One technician said that being sent off-site was viewed as a bonus: "It's kind of like a reward once in a while for busting your butt." Technicians appear to get the training they need, but are sometimes hampered by lack of manpower. If a technician is scheduled to work when a technical class is being held during the work day, he must find someone to cover for him. One manager felt that training was less successful in this group because of recent growth and subsequent manpower shortages.

The firm also uses dedicated trainers and outside consultants to provide general training. One trainer conducts a "frontline leadership" program for workers, supervisors, and managers, as well as a program to teach problem-solving skills. When the firm first transitioned to TQM a few years ago, outside consultants provided training, but with mixed success. Whereas some line staff received training in just-in-time management and in cell layout, the consultant appeared to ignore other groups. MPM now has a designated in-house trainer to develop these programs.

By and large, employees at all levels felt that the transition to new work practices and the training received were successful and resulted in good problem-solving skills at all levels. Some noted shortcomings in supervisors' training. Management recognizes that the company is still in transition and could identify specific stumbling blocks. The notion of continuous improvement, for example, can be hard to grasp because it requires a change in thinking: training is not down time or "a waste, but something to be proud of." Likewise, TQM training is still idiosyncratic across factories, sometimes "cosmetic" (e.g., managers, but not frontline workers, get plaques) and prevalent for the top third of the workforce (including some team leaders, but not frontline workers).

## HEALTH AGENCY

Like MPM, the health agency (HA) has adopted TQM and continuous quality improvement (CQI) approaches to meet its goal of providing quality health care in the most cost-effective way. An important way to reduce costs and improve quality of care is to reduce hospital stays and provide post-discharge support and skilled care for patients in the home. This shift from hospital to home care affects the work and training needs of many staff, including the home health aides and licensed vocational nurses (LVNs) that were the subjects of our study. In addition, health agencies are subject to a variety of regulations and oversight that affect their staff assignments and training requirements.

The HA administration envisions many changes in home health that affect the aides and LVNs. For example, while home health has traditionally been seen as the end point of some plan of care, typically beginning with a hospital stay, the new conception marks home health as a "transition" point that can occur at various times. Thus, patients may go from an emergency room visit to home without being admitted for a hospital stay at all. As care and patient education increase in the home setting, and as the number of patients at home increases, cost-effectiveness issues are inevitably raised. HA has determined that one way to increase efficiency and productivity is to shift personnel costs by giving more home care tasks to LVNs and aides, while limiting nurses' responsibilities to initial assessment/intake and discharge.

The HA management realizes that increasing LVNs in home health is not a popular move with the nurses' union. The union is always involved when the home care division wants to change work rules.[3] It is expected that the nurses' union "takes everything on." When management wanted to increase productivity by requiring 25 home visits per week, for example, they expected grievances and subsequent negotiations.

The question at the core of the debate is whether LVNs can provide the same quality of care as RNs:

> "We don't have enough work for LVNs primarily because RNs aren't willing to give up some of the things they've always done. They don't assign the appropriate patients to the LVN... The only thing an RN has to do is the admission and discharge assessment. LVNs can do everything else, by law."

While HA management is confident that it can train advanced nursing and certify LVNs and, in some cases, aides, to administer to patients' needs, nurses, not surprisingly, are uneasy about such changes. Even though this plan is more cost-effective, they see a trend "to send sicker and sicker people back home," and not enough "highly trained people" (e.g., nurses) to treat them. For their part, the aides and LVNs we talked to felt capable of performing more tasks, given proper training.

We cannot speculate on the outcome of this particular struggle. And whether or not the mix of staff providing home care changes, the HA recognizes many training challenges to shift the perception and role of home health care in the overall plan of care, to implement TQM and CQI processes, and to keep up with technology changes that affect home care, such as electronic blood and cholesterol monitors.

On the positive side, training in the health industry is commonly accepted as part of doing business. The HA provides continuous

---

[3]HA has dealings with 11 unions. Two are involved in proposed changes in the home care division—the nurses' union and the service employees' union. A 10-week nurses' strike in 1990 produced bad feelings, which apparently still affect management-union relations. We made several attempts to interview union representatives for this study, but were unsuccessful in gaining their participation. As a result, this discussion reflects management's views alone.

training opportunities for all levels of the workforce to meet both individual job and institutional certification.  Management training is supported through orientation classes and a variety of courses.  Mandatory training, such as in cardiopulmonary resuscitation (CPR), varies according to the type of staff.  Doctors and emergency room staff, for example, receive mandatory training in "advanced cardiac life," pediatric staff in "pediatric advanced cardiac life."  Home health workers—aides and LVNs—have both elective and mandatory educational activities.  Many classes or seminars (e.g., on documentation or Medicare guidelines) are videotaped so that absent staff can make up any that are missed.  The HA offers language classes, a 12-week cultural awareness course (taught by university professors), and, after one year of employment, reimburses other education through a tuition reimbursement program.  Training is also tied to career development programs for nurses, aides, and other staff.

Total quality improvement (TQI) staff are developing methods to assess the impact of training programs.  At present, staff are designing a project to determine the skills they plan to train and examine the extent to which skills are being used and procedures implemented.  TQI staff meet monthly with the home health department to reinforce the TQI process.

## Selection and Hiring

The health agency is reorganizing under conditions of austerity and, as a result, are simultaneously hiring, training, and downsizing.  The home health director sets standards in line with certification and licensure requirements; department supervisors interview applicants at the LVN or aide level.  Human resources personnel verify an applicant's qualifications for the job posting.  Aides require one year of home care experience and a medical/surgical certification, usually completed through coursework at an adult school.  LVNs generally complete a one-year program based on an acute care model.  Aides need a specified number of hours per year of continuing education to maintain their certification.  The home care providers we interviewed found their current jobs through newspaper ads and internal job postings.

Although the department supervisor has latitude in hiring part-time staff, for full-time staff she is bound by union seniority rules, which can be "frustrating." Unions also determine wages, which are tied to seniority, not performance.[4]

Working within union constraints (e.g., rules applying to seniority or hiring of temporary workers), the home health division management says they take a long-term view toward acquiring and developing staff. The HA has relationships with magnet schools and career academy programs in local high schools, and encourages employees to use the tuition reimbursement program to upgrade skills.

## Training for Home Health Providers

A dedicated HA training department provides a variety of training services for home health workers. The HA establishes the budget, but senior staff in home health have an indirect influence on its determination. The HA is in a period of transition, and many operations and processes are going through review, including the training programs. As at MPM, the tensions that naturally accompany organizational change are evident here.

The designated trainer is developing new training programs for aides and LVNs to meet quality care objectives. When the trainer began this task a few years ago, the home health staff had been conducting its own needs assessments and training rather than taking part in the division training programs. The perception was that home health was "out of the loop"—department management did not want to work with the trainer or permit staff to attend education programs designed for them. In addition, the person charged to coordinate education and training left and was not replaced.

A management shakeup has turned this around, although the trainer has had to overcome low staff motivation created, in the view of several respondents, by previous poor management and disappointment with the recently negotiated union contract. When the trainer did get involved, several problems were identified in the policies and

---

[4]This appears problematic for implementing CQI; if salaries are linked to seniority, then supervisors' performance assessments have little impact.

procedures, as well as gaps in continuing education for staff. Although cooperation has improved and the training program is on track, the trainer finds that staff vary in their responsiveness to training, and departments must often mandate training to ensure participation.  When she asked for volunteers for pediatric patient training, for example, only one person showed up.  One strategy she has adopted is to conduct education activities in conjunction with regular staff meetings whenever possible.  This strategy seems to boost attendance in training sessions.

As mentioned above, new training programs are geared to quality goals.  Home health aides, for example, take a class in providing home care for coronary artery bypass graft (CABG) patients.  The average length of hospital stay for patients having coronary bypass, open heart surgery has been reduced to about four days.  Patients have "very high acuity" when they go home because most are over 60 and need follow-up, especially in their wound care.  The trainer had very high attendance at this training because "they were clamoring for that." Aides without critical care experience are "more fearful" of this kind of patient: "it freaks them out to think this guy just had an open heart, and already is home."  The training builds their confidence in caring for these patients.

As new programs are being designed to meet needs and requirements, staff must simultaneously grapple with effects of downsizing in their work, including their ability to supervise students.  At the same time, they are looking ahead to providing cross-training to LVNs to expand their skills and responsibilities in providing health care.

As new hires, LVNs receive training in CPR, fire and safety, a week-long orientation, and service enrichment (i.e., "how to be nice to your patients").  The department provides on-the-job training, 20 percent of which is general training and 80 percent is department-specific.  LVN department administration conducts performance evaluations, which are generic, criteria-based evaluations that are coordinated throughout the region.  These evaluations can also be modified to apply to home health aides.

The training program for aides is linked to a career path, which proceeds as follows:  aide/registered nurse assistant (RNA), clinic assistant, LVN, registered nurse (RN), and registered nurse practitioner (RNP). The HA supports the training programs, which are coordinated with local colleges, and may include work internships at HA as part of the program. These are offered on a tuition reimbursement basis, with departments targeting individuals for career development. There is typically a waiting list for these classes and, because of staff reductions, the HA currently offers fewer classes than it has in the past.

Aides and LVNs in our sample were positive about the training they had received in the HA. An LVN said she received a three-week orientation when she switched to home health that included accompanying a nurse, social worker, physical therapist, and occupational therapist on their patient rounds. She has taken a variety of courses offered by the training department, which are advertised through memos. The aide also received extensive in-service training when she was hired, and has attended several day-long classes. She is planning to take more classes now that she qualifies for reimbursement. During the first year of employment, new staff must take these courses on their own time.

## TRAFFIC MANAGEMENT

Traffic management agencies are coping with technology changes that affect technical skill needs for the entire industry. The most significant change has been from electro-mechanical to digital systems. Although traffic signal technicians still need mechanical skills to work with older equipment, they need technical skills related to computer-based signals, controllers, and the like. Newer technologies such as fiber optics, cellular telecommunications, and microwave are gradually being introduced into traffic signal management systems.

Despite significant changes in technology and agency liability for maintenance, public agencies responsible for traffic signals have no budget for training programs. Our study focused on traffic signal technician work in one city government (Agency A), but we also interviewed staff responsible for training in a neighboring larger city (Agency B) and in the county that houses them (Agency C). As we elaborate below, selection and hiring practices can hamper an agency's ability to obtain the skills it needs (Agency B), or they can be part of a strategy to obtain needed skills without providing training (Agency A).

Traffic signals are owned by jurisdictions, which have responsibility for traffic signal maintenance and can be held liable when failed signals contribute to traffic mishaps. Eighty-eight different jurisdictions, most of which are cities or incorporated areas, have this responsibility in the Los Angeles metropolitan area. Jurisdictions can hire other public or private agencies to maintain their signals, or they can staff a designated workforce to maintain their own. The city that was the focus of our investigation (Agency A) maintained its own signals and also did contract work for other jurisdictions. Agency A has a reputation for being on the cutting edge of technology advances in the field and for being a "training ground."

## Selection and Hiring

As public entities attached to local governments, all three agencies are subject to civil service rules and requirements in their selection and hiring practices. But the civil service's impact on each is somewhat distinct.

**Agency A.** The manager of Agency A, the smallest site, has to write a justification for a position, which civil service must approve (and can eliminate during a budget shortfall). Applicants take a test, which assesses basic electrical and electronic knowledge, for two classifications—assistant traffic signal technician, level I and level II. Once hired, assistant techs must take certain courses at the local city college (or one of their choice) and on-the-job training (OJT, discussed below). When a technician position opens, level I or II assistant techs must "compete with all the outside world for the next position up." In reality, though, only one tech in the shop had been brought in above the assistant tech level.

According to management, the qualifying technician's test is very difficult. It includes questions about computers, electrical material, and traffic signals as well as practical tests that involve solving problems using schematics. In the past, experienced technicians with associate degrees have tested better than inexperienced candidates with a degree in electrical engineering.

When a position is open, the agency advertises in newspapers. The manager writes job descriptions that emphasize electronics skills and working on electronics devices while deemphasizing traffic signals, which many technicians still associate with electrical systems.

The agency's preference is to bring in people at the assistant level, train them, and, over time, promote from within. Respondents at all three agencies emphasized OJT as a skill development strategy, in part because technical education specific to traffic signals is not offered in education and training institutions. At most, agencies can identify prospective employees with coursework or degrees in electronics or digital systems.

**Agency B.** In a much larger nearby city, Agency B is hampered by out-of-date civil service classifications, which it has been trying to change for seven years. The current classification for traffic signal electrician is very broad and includes different jobs and various skill levels (e.g., construction electricians who install equipment, maintenance technicians who maintain it, and emergency traffic signal electricians who respond to emergency calls). Applicants take a general test: only about 15 percent of the questions assess electrical knowledge relevant to the job. Supervisors say that civil service is not testing directly for technician skills because "they are afraid of a challenge by all different groups that it's not work-related." The civil service rule, according to respondents, is that a skill not utilized by 50 percent of a class in the last 90 days cannot be tested for. Because civil service is responsible for validating skill requirements included on the exam, and because it is expensive to create a new exam, civil service is reluctant to break up the classification (respondents stated that the cost of reclassification in this case would be $70,000).

Agency B would like to change the classification to system signal technician, "so that we can require a minimum of two years of electronics at our journeyman trade school." Managers said the current test fails to identify appropriate applicants in two ways. First, because the test is general, applicants who pass it may not have requisite electronics skills, and second:

> "We don't get people taking the exam because when you read the exam requirements, you don't see it (electronics) there. It's not even mentioned."

Agency B can interview only those applicants who pass the exam. Agency B staff felt they "can find the people [they need] if they allow us to write the description of the job." In their view, the local labor market has an abundance of digital techs and computer techs who lost jobs with the decline of the aerospace industry and who are good candidates for training in traffic signals.

Because the test is the gate to an interview for outside applicants, Agency B tries to "mine the internal job market" to find qualified technicians. The Department of Water and Power (DWP), for example, was a source of candidates for Agency B because DWP had an internal training program and "had no problem educating their people—even to the fact that they might lose them." Agency B admits, "we don't have much control over it [the internal job market]," because there are few incentives for the more qualified technicians to move. Technicians in Agency B make less money than, for example, similarly skilled staff in DWP: because DWP is revenue-generating, it maintains higher pay scales.

**Agency C.** The county in which the previous two city agencies reside has a classification for a digital systems electrician/technician that it can advertise and test for. The test emphasizes electronics, not signals, and applicants must achieve a 70 percent passing score to advance to an interview. Previously, the classification was traffic signal technician, and emphasized electro-mechanic skills at the journeyman level. It was able to get a title change by borrowing digital systems techs from another department. Agency C froze hiring under the old title, and now attracts and hires individuals with the skills they need.

Generally speaking, all three agencies adopt a "grow-your-own" strategy, and feel the labor market has an adequate pool of workers to select from. But because specific skills can be learned only on the job, experienced traffic signal technicians are at a premium. Agency A, which has the most sophisticated technology, loses techs to higher-paying positions in other jurisdictions. All three are understaffed but, with the exception of Agency B, are not able to hire.[5]

---

[5]At the time of our interview, Agency B was hiring eight technicians because the city received Federal Emergency Management Assistance (FEMA) after the January 1994 Northridge earthquake.

Unlike the health industry, certification is not required for traffic signal work. Agency A requires new techs to obtain a level I certification from the International Municipal Signal Association (IMSA). Techs must pay for and take required courses on their own time. The supervisor felt IMSA "is becoming mandatory." A tech who worked for Agency C had a level III certification which, though not required, he had completed on his own time.

> "I just figured . . . every group in whatever industry you're in has their own certification classes. If you don't have it, some day you'll be required to get it."

A growing concern about litigation was also cited as a reason to encourage certification:

> "I see it also as a coming thing . . . as attorneys bring litigation against the cities and counties for malfunctioning signals."

Lack of certification was not seen as a problem. Rather, if someone was certified, it indicated he had more training. Having a certification could improve a job seeker's employment chances over one who was not certified.

> "If you can say, well, they've been certified, then somehow that seems to put an extra stamp of quality . . . insurance on the work, whether it is relevant or not."

In this industry, then, certification is desirable in case of litigation and indicative of a technician's training or motivation—techs in each agency have to pay for coursework themselves. There is no pay incentive to becoming certified: in Agency A, techs who were hired before level I certification became mandatory have little incentive to obtain it.

## Training Traffic Signal Technicians

**Agency A.** A traffic signal technician in Agency A described his training as follows:

> "What they did was, they brought me in the office . . . this current job is technician, not electrician . . . They asked me, 'do you know

how to turn an intersection on that's on flash?' I said, 'yes, I stop-time the controller in yellow for the slow phase and as soon as the traffic's clear, I turn it on and turn off the stop-timer.' They said, 'fine, you're going to start as a technician on Monday.' That was my training. There was none. They just wanted to make sure I wouldn't kill somebody when I turned on the intersection. They figure you'll learn as you go."

Traffic signal department management describes its policy as continuous OJT that begins as soon as someone is hired. There are four levels of work: maintenance assistant, traffic signal assistant, traffic signal electrician, and traffic signal technician. Most techs work up these four levels and can advance when an opening exists and the budget allows it. New and experienced techs begin out in the field with electricians and assist with "labor work"—laying conduit, digging trenches, setting poles—to learn:

how the thing goes together in the field—even if you hire a guy off the street for a technician, he still has to learn [this]. That's one of the reasons we like to get them as an assistant, because we're not paying them as much to learn the same thing.

The field experience and OJT approach is necessary because technicians may have knowledge of electronics or digital systems, but no direct experience with traffic signals. Even for experienced workers, they "don't like to take people from other cities with bad habits. We would rather grow our own techs."

A department supervisor has taken on training responsibilities as part of his job. He has been asked to put together a curriculum and a training plan that will standardize training somewhat but, because of other responsibilities, he can work on it only sporadically during the day or after work hours on his own time.

The technicians themselves note that management has enough money to buy new equipment, but not enough to teach them how to use it: "The only thing we've had is free seminars by vendors." One technician volunteered to use vacation time to take a class in fiber optics if Agency A would pay tuition; it refused. A supervisor acknowledged that some companies have good seminars on their products, but the department does not have the budget to send the techs or the manpower to let someone off work to attend them.

If the equipment has a service contract, it can be sent back to the vendor for repairs. But service contracts are typically not purchased, both for cost-cutting reasons and because technicians are expected to be able to fix the equipment. If technicians are not trained to use new equipment or if it breaks down, they "fiddle around" with the machine when they have time. Technicians felt this policy had mixed effects. It may be cheaper to replace the equipment than for inexperienced techs to attempt to repair it. On the positive side, repairing equipment helps technicians learn how it really operates.[6]

The policy of having techs repair equipment—and relatedly, not to throw anything out—is consistent with the technicians' community of practice in several respects. Technicians are "tinkerers" and problem solvers who are challenged by having to figure out solutions to problems and regularly discuss problems and solutions with their colleagues. "Tailgate" meetings are held biweekly to share knowledge developed on the job. If something comes up between meetings, techs meet informally in the shop at the beginning of the day. Technicians freely seek help from each other, as needed: one described OJT as "spur-of-the-moment and self-initiated." Thus, the community of practice supports the development of technicians' skills in the absence of formal training or structured OJT.

Although Agency A has state-of-the-art technology, it is not necessarily utilized in technicians' work, in part because training is inadequate. The push to purchase new technology, which contributes to the department's reputation as an innovator, has several motives. One is management's belief that technology can improve traffic management. (Recall the description of the "control room," for example, in Chapter Three.) Another reason voiced by employees is to maintain job security. If the city government perceives that the technology is vital to the traffic management operation and that a skilled workforce is needed to support technology utilization, then it will be less inclined to contract the work out to private companies or other agencies. Finally, managers could find political support for

---

[6]Training can make a difference in whether technology is utilized. Both MPM and Agency A have fluke testers, a multifaceted electronic testing device. At MPM, where training is provided, the equipment is in use; at Agency A the same machine stands idle because the tech trained to use it left the agency.

technology investment because politicians see such investments as a positive change that they want to be associated with.

**Agency B.** In Agency B, the Department of Transportation's (DOT's) manual of policies and procedures and official job descriptions give supervisors—first-level line managers—responsibility for training their staff, but no budget to do so. The DOT's position is that formal training is not necessary because it is a journeyman job class, and anyone hired into it is expected to be a journeyman who was fully trained by the union. The group we interviewed had two field staff designated as trainers, who could not be replaced with new hires. Instead, the department had two fewer staff to do the same amount of work. The supervisors received permission for this arrangement by arguing that trainers were needed for liability reasons. Management agreed, as long as the department was still able to get its work done with reduced staff. A supervisor said there is always funding for tuition reimbursement if a tech wants to pursue outside training on his own, but no funds for technical training or equipment upgrades. Classes for using the new computers were cut after a budget crunch. He described this situation as "frustrating":

> "Is this any way to run a business? I think that's a problem . . . that we, that many of us continue to go to school in the private sector, and we know about the management principles, the way things are being done. And we come back here, and we just hit our head against the wall."

Agency B used to have a job rotation scheme, with staff rotating every six months. But staffing cuts have reduced its ability to continue this. Fortunately, rotation is less necessary now because Agency B has standardized the technology somewhat: it now uses only three types of controllers instead of 27.

Despite few resources for training, Agency B says its strategy is to build a labor force internally through OJT, job rotation, and mandatory in-house technical classes. Classes held on company time help ensure attendance by both apprentices (craft helpers) and journeymen. "Maintenance" labor can attend by invitation, either on their own or by a supervisor's recommendation, but must have permission to take the class during work hours. Even mandatory attendance does not ensure training, however, because emergencies always take precedence and because Agency B is currently under-staffed.[7] Similarly, supervisors cannot spare maintenance workers who show promise for advancement and want to attend class.

Supervisors tell workers who are interested in promotion to take outside classes on their own. The department will reimburse course tuition, but not books, if the worker passes the class. This reimbursement covers about half of the costs. In addition, wage policies (discussed earlier) discourage worker investment in outside training.

**Agency C.** In Agency C, the repair lab has taken over the function of the training group for the bureau and is responsible for training some 140 employees. Its OJT aims to upgrade employee expertise "from whatever it was to a higher level. We're not going to bring everyone to the same level—whatever that is—but they will all benefit. We evaluate them as we go along and feed them the technical as they can handle it."

The policy is to hire digital systems electricians or technicians and train them in signals. There is no separate budget for training. Once a person is hired, a rotation is set up so the employee works for six months in each shop (except for a year in the signal shop). After two rotations—about two years—the individual is evaluated and placed "where he's most productive or where he'd like to work." There are exceptions to this rotation scheme, however: one technician said he spent little time in the field and did not work in construction at all.

Agency C attempts to assess skill needs and offers training classes. A systems technician who interfaces between the shop and the field to oversee special projects will report back to the supervisor when he perceives weaknesses or areas for improvement. In his view, there is "no way to get the information to people unless you tack something up and give a class." Since "technology changes occur yearly in this industry," ongoing classes are important.

> "We don't expect them to know everything, but we expect them to be responsible. And if they get to a point where there is doubt in

---

[7]State guidelines suggest a ratio of 60 signals per worker, and the industrial standard (U.S. Association of Traffic Signals) is 35 per worker. The three agencies have significantly higher signal-to-technician ratios: Agency A reports 120–150:1, Agency B, 150:1, and Agency C, 75:1.

their mind because of the nature of our business, stop and call someone."

Thus, the community of practice encourages workers to ask questions and share solutions, thereby increasing the likelihood that technicians will acquire the knowledge, skills, and attitudes they need on the job. Whether reliance on informal OJT substitutes for planned OJT or training classes remains an open question. But the prevailing view of traffic signal technical staff in our three sites was one of frustration over lack of organizational commitment to training and resignation that they must do the best they can with limited training resources.

## TRANSPORTATION AGENCY

The transportation agency's mission is to build and operate a coordinated transportation system in the Los Angeles region. The cost and scope of the project place TA operations under scrutiny by the public and the press and subject it to political pressures. Two changes—a merger and adoption of TQM in one division—have hampered hiring and training in the agency itself, but affect inspection jobs only indirectly.

The recent merger and subsequent reduction in the workforce (through both layoffs and voluntary separations) decimated the human resources department and any former training capacity. The merger brought together two agencies with different training philosophies. One invested in staff training (conflict resolution, performance evaluations, safety, staff and skills development, and management training for middle management were mentioned), while the other provided only basic word processing and computer training. Agency staff and others feel that training is not a priority, but is the first item to be cut when budgets are tight. The following comments about training are illustrative:

"If there is [a human resources strategy], management has not disseminated it."

"When the agency restructured, they moved in people to HR who had no training experience or knowledge. In this way, the program was set up to fail."

Formerly, department heads set and requested budgets for training. Now, except for specialized programs, training is centrally consolidated and department heads must request funds. Human resources staff report that recent requests have been turned down. The exception is department requests for TQM-related training funds, which have been set aside to advance TQM implementation.

The agency is beginning to implement TQM in one division, but the associated training has been sparse and limited to managers in the agency or in contractor firms. Although agency departments can request funds for TQM trainers for their own staff, any TQM-related training for survey and construction inspectors working for contractors is described as "in the queue." TQM practices, then, are neither widespread nor uniform across the agency and the contracting firms. The contractor who hires the construction inspectors, for example, had initiated a quality program of its own before the transportation agency adopted TQM. But their quality assurance manager felt that training had had little impact thus far, in part because training classes aimed at all employees had fallen behind schedule. Although TQM training is only "percolating" at lower levels of the workforce, it is "the most concentrated effort at enhancing worker productivity that is taking place [in the transportation agency] at this time."[8]

---

[8]The TA also has special programs designed to help train the current and future workforce. The Job Development Training Program (JDTP), for example, began with economic development funds received by the city to help rebuild after a period of civil unrest. The TA commissioner wanted to provide more employment opportunities and to hire the unemployed. Funds for JDTP will come from the contractors, whose contract stipulates that 3 percent of direct labor costs must be set aside for training purposes. A consultant was hired to work with the contractors to develop a plan. JDTP, which is still in the planning stages, will target some training resources for unemployed, minority individuals, ages 17–25, for jobs in construction inspection, and to increase technical skills of incumbent workers. The agency also supports school-to-careers programs at several high schools to help prepare students for transportation-related careers. These programs are aimed more toward professional occupations—such as architecture, urban planning, and engineering—than at sub-B.A. technical jobs. Several respondents said these activities were not part of a strategic plan, but result from efforts of a single individual who has successfully pursued grants to support educational development projects.

Overall, we conclude that training in the transportation agency—apart from fledgling TQM-related efforts—is more ad hoc than planned. The agency merger is apparently one reason: "[we are] still trying to blend the agency at the nuts and bolts level." In addition, the traditional view of human resources may reflect the agency's focus on whether transportation needs are being met. As one trainer observed: "the incentive in the public sector is to get the job done, not to train." In this respondent's view, the private sector can and does have trainers to develop the labor pool, and it can assume the risks associated with training investments. The public sector, on the other hand, may be less willing to do so.

## Selection and Hiring

Study respondents expressed various opinions about the supply and quality of the inspector workforce. In one experienced manager's view, the home-building industry, which employs craft workers in the construction trades, had been hard-hit in the recent economic recession. Consequently, pools of qualified, unemployed workers sit in union halls waiting to be hired. Although required skills do not completely overlap, he thought the transition from home-building to rail construction was relatively easy. A trainer for a construction firm, however, saw a "skills gap" because inspector skills for the building trades and transportation only partly overlap. The trainer noted that the large firms that hold the major contracts have the training infrastructure to close this gap, whereas smaller subcontractors may not.[9]

Whether or not a "skills gap" exists, we conclude that the agency and contractors must concern themselves with the public's *perception* of quality and, relatedly, liability. When a worker has an accident or when a roadway collapses over a subway tunnel that's under construction, quality is questioned. Certification is a way to improve public relations and perhaps afford some protection if something goes wrong.

---

[9]The agency's decision to train inspectors through the JDTP initiative is based on an "educated guess" about future needs, not on a formal job market analysis. At least one manager felt this was short-sighted and expressed concern over trainees' ability to find jobs.

The agency can encourage the construction firms to hire certified inspectors, but this is not currently a contractual requirement. TA managers felt that "folks are reasonably cooperative" in hiring certified inspectors—the firms have an incentive to comply with TA requests because the construction contracts are worth several million dollars and the competition among firms is high.[10]  A TA manager described the situation as "nip and tuck"—while safety training is mandatory, the provision of even basic training to frontline workers varies from firm to firm. Agency management, construction managers, and inspectors themselves recognize that certification standards are not uniform and not necessarily linked to better performance on the job. They also recognize that certification is limited because it only covers basic skills and knowledge; in-house training is needed to ensure quality inspections that reflect the requirements of specific sites.

The firm requires new job incumbents and inspectors from other fields to take classes at a local skills center to prepare for certification exams. A manager keeps track of their progress. This company is also developing question-and-answer study guidelines for the test in reinforced concrete building code. They also require all workers and welder and concrete inspectors to be certified by the American Concrete Institute and American Welding Institute. The company pays tuition costs for the classes, and will bring instructors in. The company covers part of the time required to attend classes; the remainder must be taken as personal time.

Not surprisingly, quality assurance (QA) managers who work for TA and the subway contract manager encourage certification even among experienced transportation inspectors. Their concern seems related, in part, to the nature of the labor market. As one manager noted, most inspectors are former craftsmen who became skilled in a particular trade. A craftsman's "mind-set" is "to get in and get out." As an inspector, the former craftsman has a much different role; he must ensure that contractors do the required work. Whereas craftsmen look for shortcuts, good inspectors know about shortcuts and look for them.  Another QA manager felt that inspectors had

---

[10]The agency plans to make certification a requirement in future contracts. Presently, they encourage 90 percent of the staff to hold appropriate certifications.

"mediocre qualifications" because contractors are typically more concerned with making money than with hiring qualified inspectors, and because only about 65 percent of their current workforce hold certifications, some of which are unrelated to current job responsibilities. Rather than seek the most qualified, contractors depend on their internal labor market and a set of inspectors who move from job to job.

Certification is not a salient issue for survey inspectors. Union training leads to certification, but it is not required to hold a job as a survey inspector. One party chief, for example, had taken requisite union classes, but not certification tests. These inspectors worked for a smaller, family-owned company, where personal contacts played a part in hiring decisions. The chief had previously worked for his supervisor (a nephew of the owner) and was offered the job when it became available. Similarly, the rod man sought out several firm owners in the area after passing his apprenticeship test. When a position opened up, "this firm knew him."[11]

Union membership and the licensing exam are the "ticket[s] to practice" in the survey profession, where the union sets wages[12] and training policies, which help structure OJT (discussed below). Construction inspectors, although they do not belong to a union, work in a union context. Unions involved with TA's contractors pay the prevailing wage and have agreed not to strike. Compared with home health, the relationship between unions and management in the transportation agency seems more cooperative.

## Training Inspectors

**Construction Inspectors.** Individual (construction or construction management) firms and their subcontractors are responsible for training inspectors. Contractors formed a consortium for planning, training, and staff hiring. The firm in charge of subway construction

---

[11]And when the firm had to downsize from three to two crews, the staff who stayed on "were not the best," according to surveyors, but those who had been with the company longer.

[12]According to a supervisor, union surveyors earn 50 percent more than do non-union surveyors in California, and twice as much as prevailing union wages in some other states.

management (construction inspectors) has an in-house training staff and also hires outside consultants. Currently, training on the job is informal and supervised by lead inspectors. The company provides training to meet safety requirements (e.g., hazardous materials handling) and for certifications related to job-specific skills (e.g., American Concrete Institute). Workers learn about these courses from the trainer or at chief inspector meetings.

As TQM practices trickle down to the frontline workforce, training has begun to emphasize quality goals. For example, the company is in the process of developing training modules to be used in the field that will help standardize how inspectors should do their job on site. The goal is to improve uniformity of inspections across job sites. The emphasis is still on job-specific training—tailored to the specialty and the specifications of the job site—but cross-training is increasingly encouraged. One senior inspector, for example, reported receiving training sessions in six different construction areas—electrical, mechanical equipment, utilities, cathodic protection, masonry, and heating and ventilation equipment.

According to the construction inspectors, company management has been eager to provide training and job orientation and to answer questions. The inspectors believe these practices help develop worker expertise. They view OJT as essential to the job. Supervisors are kept up to date through continuous training provided primarily by the resident engineer for each construction segment.

**Survey Inspectors.** Training for survey inspectors is a combination of union-provided training, on-the-job training in line with professional standards, and formal classes to meet mandatory requirements, such as safety-related training.

Training for survey inspectors is integrated with their standards of professional practice. Following professional tradition, which is tied to union policy, the party chief and the crew supervisor are responsible for training apprentices to become journeymen chain men and for chain men to advance to party chief. New surveyors can learn "academics" from formal schooling, including the union school, but on-the-job training is crucial to developing expertise in the field. This emphasis on OJT supports the way surveyors define the nature of their work—as constant problem solving geared to the unique characteristics of each work setting. The supervisor and crew members emphasize "constant teaching" and learning as important aspects of their job.

In addition to OJT, surveyors may attend occasional training seminars conducted by equipment vendors or classes sponsored by the union. Workers are satisfied with union training, but tend to avoid vendor seminars because they take too much time for the information presented and are usually followed by a sales pitch. As one inspector said, "I could read a book to get the needed information."

When new technology is adopted at the worksite, the supervisor expects crew members to read the manual and learn to "figure it out" on the job. Again, this practice is described as "tradition," because the pool of surveyors is small and it is not cost-effective to offer special courses. This practice was accepted by the survey crew and stands in contrast to the expectation of traffic signal technicians, who expressed frustration at having to teach themselves how to use new technology purchased by management.[13]

Like the traffic signal technicians, the survey inspectors are members of a community of practice that supports on-the-job training in the absence of formal training. But we note some important differences. First, survey inspectors clearly articulate notions of professionalism and tradition and their importance in carrying out the work they do. Their strong sense of professionalism permeates discussions about training, working as part of a team, and meeting quality performance standards. Traffic signal technicians, on the other hand, emphasize their individual expertise. Practices like "tailgate meetings" or asking questions when help is needed are in place to support a weak system—where training is not valued once hired, and where job rotation policies to promote cross-training and the development of expertise are lax.

---

[13]One survey inspector, however, while accepting of the present policy, feels that firms should invest more in training and apprenticeships in order to keep up with future technology changes, such as those that will capitalize on the Global Positioning System. In his view, firms need to overcome the fear that training will lead workers to leave for other jobs. Rather, "workers leave because they are unappreciated."

# Chapter Six

# CONCLUSIONS AND IMPLICATIONS

This study demonstrates that work context matters in the consideration of skills. Workplaces are complex, dynamic social systems that defy simplistic categorization of skills and straightforward matching of skill requirements to jobs. The study provides a rich picture of skills and dispositions in the workplace, and offers the following general findings:

- Generic skills—problem solving, working in teams, communication—and dispositions are important in work and to workers.

- Generic skills and dispositions vary with work context.

- Employers do not necessarily understand the skill requirements of their frontline workforce.

- Employers may lack effective strategies for acquiring workforce skills.

- Employers do little to foster skill development among nonmanagerial workers and sometimes take courses of action that undermine skill development.

- Employers have weak connections with education providers for supporting acquisition or development of workforce skills.

Although our sample of jobs and worksites is small, the issues raised in this research are not unique to these cases. Many organizations are grappling with changes in the business environment and feel pressures to respond. Many believe that they need workers with different kinds of skills than in the past and feel frustrated that educational institutions are not preparing individuals to face the challenges presented in the modern workplace. The conclusions we draw, then, can provide interesting and instructive examples from which others can learn.

The following sections recap our main findings and conclusions and draw implications for school reform, skill standards, and further research. One theme that arises repeatedly is the tension between different conceptions of skills and skill requirements. Public policy and discourse about skills remain rooted in a conception of skill requirements that downplays or ignores the work context. By taking a sociocultural approach to the problem, we hope to illuminate the limitations of research and policy that do not take sociocultural perspectives into account. This is one step toward expanding the public policy discourse.

## GENERIC SKILLS AND DISPOSITIONS ARE IMPORTANT IN WORK, BUT VARY BY WORK CONTEXT

The concepts of generic skills and work-related dispositions, as defined in this report, are salient to the workers, supervisors, and managers who took part in this study. Skills such as communications, problem solving, working as part of a team, and positive dispositions toward work are readily observed across different jobs, and, according to study participants, are essential to effective performance.

However, whereas generic skills and dispositions are identifiable in all jobs, their specific characteristics and importance vary among jobs. The characteristics of problem solving, teamwork, communication, and disposition are related to job demands, which in turn depend on the purpose of the work, the tasks that constitute the job, the organization of the work, and other aspects of the work context.

The fact that generic skills and dispositions vary has several implications for employers. One concerns job candidate selection. The available survey data indicate that employers believe that generic skills and dispositions (referred to as attitudes in most employer surveys) are important, and they place a high value on such skills in choosing among job candidates (NCEQW, 1995; Cappelli and Rogowsky, 1995). According to the most recent national survey, employers making hiring decisions rated an applicant's communication skills and attitudes higher than previous work experience, employer recommendations, industry-based credentials, and several schooling variables (e.g., tests, academic performance, teacher recommendations) (NCEQW, 1995).

These survey findings suggest that employers use general capacities like "communication" and "attitudes" as a screen to distinguish between job candidates. In comparison to other available evidence that employers might have, such as degrees earned, previous experience, teacher recommendations, and so on, "communication skills" and "attitudes" are not only more subjective, but employers can presumably assess them only during a face-to-face job interview. Our study, however, shows that communication skills or dispositions actually employed on the job can be very specific—for example, the negotiation skills exhibited by construction inspectors or the bedside manners of home health workers—and that they are strongly context dependent. "Communication" in an interview, then, seems a weak indicator of communications skills potentially employed on the job.

If employers want to use "communication" or "attitudes" as indicators of a job applicant's suitability, it makes sense to replace these broad, ambiguous terms with more specific descriptions. Better information about skills on the job can presumably be used to construct a finer screen, but would require employers to possess deeper knowledge about "communications" and "attitudes" in the work context. In our study, some employers had such knowledge and used it in an interview setting to screen applicants. Managers and supervisors of traffic signal technicians, for example, sought candidates who liked to used their hands and to solve problems. They reported asking job candidates if they worked on their own car, operated ham radios, or had other hobbies or interests that might show these skills. The managers we spoke to were former signal techs themselves and, like the incumbent techs we observed, identified "tinkering" as an important characteristic of a traffic signal technician. Managers who understand work practice can use that knowledge to refine hiring and selection criteria, whether such criteria are subjective or quantifiable.[1]

---

[1]This was especially important in the traffic signal technician case, because the formal hiring process defined by civil service examinations did not adequately identify candi-

Employers and trainers can also use more specific information about generic skills and dispositions to support learning on the job or to improve training practices. Employers value teamwork—but all teams do not work alike, and some teams created by workers are invisible to managers. Some teams we observed had role and knowledge interdependencies that were formalized by job designations (survey crew) or regulation (home health care), while others were created by the workers themselves (construction inspectors and test technicians). We find similar variations in the types of problem solving, communications skills, and dispositions needed to function in different jobs and in different organizations.

We conclude that very general terms like problem solving, communications, teamwork, and attitudes are too broad or ambiguous to be of much use to employers for either screening or training. Employers report that "communication skills" and "attitudes" are essential, but these terms can refer only to a job candidate's general comportment at an interview, not specific skill requirements translatable to the job.

## EMPLOYERS LACK SPECIFIC KNOWLEDGE OF WORKFORCE SKILLS AND EFFECTIVE STRATEGIES FOR ACQUIRING THEM

Our study suggests that employers do not uniformly possess accurate or useful knowledge of the skills required in their technical workforce. Managers far removed from the frontline workforce sometimes underestimate the capabilities of workers or have varying opinions about work requirements (e.g., test cell associates viewed their work as constantly changing; human resource staff called it repetitive). Transportation agency managers underestimated the capabilities of its frontline workforce to carry out planned changes to adopt TQM because they did not understand the quality control nature of inspection work.

Managers and supervisors who come up through the ranks are more articulate about specific skill requirements and have a sense of which capabilities could "make or break" success on the job (e.g., tinkerers

---

dates with appropriate job-specific knowledge, let alone job-relevant generic skills or dispositions.

make better traffic signal technicians; home health providers must accept supervision). Since generic skills and dispositions function in concert with job-specific knowledge and work context, employers with more specific knowledge can provide better information for designing instruction activities to teach skills. This has implications for school reform proposals, as discussed below.

In the firms and jobs we studied, managers generally felt that the supply of skilled labor was adequate to meet their employment needs. Selection and hiring policies, however, often constrained hiring decisions (e.g., in home health) or gave supervisors and managers little information about an applicant's job-related skills (e.g., traffic signal technicians). Some were operating under conditions of austerity that prevented any hiring at all; many departments were understaffed, with workers spread thin.

## EMPLOYERS LACK EFFECTIVE STRATEGIES FOR DEVELOPING SKILLS

Employers and employees in all the firms felt that training on the job was essential to learn the job in the first place or to keep up with the pace of change. But only two—the health care agency and the microprocessor manufacturing firm—made any significant investment in formal training. In these firms, dedicated trainers, training classes, career paths linked to acquiring higher skill levels, and other policies indicated a commitment to training.

Other firms had policies that might contribute to skill development but did not always do so. Job rotation policies to support training for traffic signal technicians were, by management's own admittance, not always followed. And techs had little regard for the few opportunities offered for vendor training, which they saw as primarily sales pitches. Policies to attain certification (for construction inspectors at TA) or to gain technical knowledge and skills (for traffic signal techs) were only partially supported through reimbursement or time off the job. Since job-related courses did not affect workers' salaries, not every tech was motivated to invest in further education and training. Managers in firms making fewer training investments—transportation construction and traffic management—expressed openly their frustration in having few training resources and seemed resigned to do what they could with what they had.

Even when formal, firm-sponsored training is absent, however, workers continue to learn on the job. Structured on-the-job training originated in the tradition of apprenticeship to prepare craft workers. In our study, OJT was carried out within communities of practice that took up the slack when formal training was not provided or failed. For survey inspectors, the training provided by the union and by other crew members on the job was the only conceivable way to learn and grow as a surveyor: surveyors believed OJT was superior to any classroom training.[2] The expectation that inspectors would train themselves (beyond what they learned in union school) was the norm for both survey inspectors and construction management. The community of practice that supported training of traffic signal technicians and construction inspectors, however, was not always visible to higher management. In some cases (e.g., signal technicians), management policies seemed to undermine rather than support an atmosphere in which experts guided newcomers in the work.

## IMPLICATIONS FOR SCHOOL REFORM

This study's findings have several implications for school reform proposals to improve youth preparation for and transition to work. Many reforms encourage closer cooperation and collaboration between education providers and employers through education-industry partnerships. Such partnerships are expected to help education providers define the knowledge and skills that new workplaces demand in order to design appropriate instructional programs. This study suggests first that employers do not uniformly possess accurate or useful knowledge of skill needs; thus the individuals who work with schools should be carefully selected. It further suggests that skills must be defined more specifically than in the past, in a way that is sensitive to differences associated with jobs and work settings. At

---

[2]This perception echoes Barley's (1995) studies of technical workers. His research suggests that much technical work resembles craft work and that "most valued skills appear to be those developed in a hands-on conversation with materials and techniques (Barley, 1995, p. 15). He refers to these as "artisanal," rather than formal, knowledge and skills.

the present time, broad teaching of workplace competencies is hampered by the lack of instructional materials that put them in the work context (SCANS, 1992) and the absence of staff development programs that help teachers learn about skills in work practice (Stasz et al., 1993).

We also note that employers in this study had weak connections to schools. They did not consider community colleges or other providers as potential sources of new technical workers. Existing relationships centered on providing job-related skills or certifications to incumbent workers (e.g., certifications for construction inspectors, technical training for traffic signal technicians). The weak link between employers and education providers in this study is similarly noted by Grubb and his colleagues in their analysis of the subbaccalaureate labor market (Grubb et al., 1992).

Some employers (and workers) were of the general opinion that American schools do a poor job or have declined since they were in school. Traffic signal technicians and their supervisors generally felt that traffic signal work was too specialized and could be learned only through experience on the job. Managers wanted employees with a background in electronics or digital systems, but did not expect any amount of school learning to substitute for learning on the job. On the other hand, they wanted technicians to take advantage of employee assistance programs to go back to school to gain more technical skills. Managers had no funds to conduct their own training, but employees could be reimbursed for taking job-related courses. Course taking was encouraged in the absence of a firm-based training strategy. Other employers (HA and TA) had partnership relationships with high schools, but these were not seen as sources for potential workers in the departments or jobs we studied.

In sum, firms generally had low regard for high school education, few connections with schools at any level, and saw no urgent reason to pursue these connections. They encouraged employees to upgrade their skills through coursework, in part as a substitute for formal job training. Our findings suggest that reforms relying on partnerships between education and industry to create a more effective U.S. education and training system may be overly ambitious. At the very least, reformers must recognize that building such partnerships may not be easy. For school-to-work reforms to become widespread it will be important to understand what incentives might encourage employers to pursue and maintain such partnerships (see Bailey, 1995).

## IMPLICATIONS FOR DEVELOPING A SKILL STANDARDS SYSTEM

The skill standards movement represents another reform effort wherein reformers hope to effect changes in education that extend to the workplace. A recent review by Bailey and Merritt (unpublished) notes the progress made thus far to develop a foundation for the development of a broader system of skill standards and raises questions about current federally funded efforts. One limitation is the approach used to identify standards: most projects relied on job-analysis methods that delineate skills and narrowly defined task lists but ignore work organization and context factors. For the most part, workers played an advisory role in the pilot projects and were often brought into the process only after a complete draft of the standards had been developed. Their job was to "validate" what was already on the list (Bailey and Merritt, unpublished). Any approaches failing to take account of the social construction of work practice will produce only partial and incomplete information about the generic skills and dispositions that employers seem to care about the most.

Another rationale behind the skill standards movement is to create a better certification system for the participating industries. A certification system can indicate to students what they must learn, provide motivation for acquiring particular skills needed in the workforce, and provide better access to a national labor market (if certifications are portable and recognized nationally). While these arguments are logical, studies of whether certification has the desired effects are lacking. Some industries have been certified for a long time—health is a good example—but research has not systematically examined how certification in these industries affects outcomes of interest, or whether *voluntary* certification—which the federal legislation supports—in different industries would have similar effects.

In our study, voluntary certification was primarily used in transportation construction to demonstrate to the public and outside critics that the workforce met some industry-defined skill standard.

According to respondents, certification reinforces the perception that workers are qualified, and this perception is important in an expensive project under constant public scrutiny such as the TA. The construction firms cooperated with the TA's desire to certify 90 percent of the workforce, but most respondents did not believe that certification affected job performance one way or the other. Industry certification was also available for survey inspectors and traffic signal technicians, but it was not required for job placement and rarely sought by workers. Further research on the current use of voluntary standards and certification may be useful to the federally funded pilot projects and other groups developing skill standards.

## IMPLICATIONS FOR FUTURE RESEARCH

The findings from this study suggest several related directions for future policy-relevant research and development, in addition to those previously mentioned. Most urgent is work that continues to explore skills and skill requirements from a sociocultural perspective, particularly in the kinds of high-performance work environments that are expected to promote productivity and economic health. Recent anthropological studies provide deeper inquiries about how people actually work and how workplaces shape work and learning, but many more are needed. Our study also suggests that particular attention be paid to the role and function of communities of practice in organizations and how they contribute to learning, standard setting, efficiency, and the like.

Further research on the role of noncognitive factors such as dispositions or interpersonal characteristics for learning and performance on the job is sorely needed. It seems essential to understand the acculturation process by which dispositions are learned or modified; the nature of this process will affect whether and how public policy has a role to play in helping to improve the acquisition and development of work-related dispositions.

At the same time, tools for measuring and assessing skills in context need to be developed. Long-term ethnographic studies are essential to build our knowledge base, but are an impractical alternative to job analysis methods. Some recent research and development efforts are exploring alternatives to traditional task and job analysis methods by examining, for example, the implications of cognitive psychology for analyzing tasks and measuring job performance (e.g., Black, 1994; Black et al., 1995; Glaser, Lesgold, and Gott, 1991). In addition, there is need for validity studies of new skill taxonomies such as those developed by SCANS or the federally funded skill standards projects that link skill standards to productivity standards. These or other research efforts should at least provide guidance for determining the differential requirements for skills across jobs, even if they cannot predict how skills (or lack of them) affect performance.

Although public education is criticized for failing to adequately prepare youth for the labor market and thereby undermining the country's ability to compete in the global economy, much less attention is paid to conditions of work and employment that also undermine competitiveness. In just the small sample of firms and jobs that we examined, several other factors besides worker skills clearly affected job performance. Since workers' skills alone can not account for any firm's shortcomings in performance, by extension, educational reform alone will not solve America's economic problems (see Barley, 1995). An important line of research is to identify problems that prevent more organizations from adopting high-performance regimes and the role of public policy in encouraging organizational changes. Appelbaum and Batt (1993), for example, discuss several policy interventions, including job training for frontline workers (not just disadvantaged workers) and incentives for encouraging unions and management to adopt more participative work systems.

Other research could explore strategies for learning and skill development that support changing work environments. Stern (1994), for example, discusses solutions to meeting high-performance goals through the strategy of just-in-time learning—"acquiring skill or knowledge at the time and place where it is needed, instead of learning it ahead of time and in a different place" (p. 2). He outlines several emerging practices in the United States and in other industrialized countries that promote employee development through just-in-time learning, including cross-training by co-workers, job rotation, skill-based pay, suggestion systems, and written analysis of work problems. Stern's approach to developing a taxonomy of practices is appealing for several reasons: (1) it offers specific, concrete suggestions for supporting skill development; (2) it offers flexibility—approaches can be implemented naturally through communities of practice and/or through more formal organizational policy (e.g., skill-based pay, written analysis of work problems); and (3) it offers a consistent way to think about learning practices in work and in other settings, such as schools.

Further consideration of how learning happens and what conditions promote it is an important direction for future research. Attention to practices that promote learning should cut across institutional boundaries—such as school and work—and across somewhat artificial distinctions such as "formal" and "informal" learning. Such distinctions currently hamper the development of education and training programs for work and lifelong learning (e.g., Resnick, 1991; Berryman, 1992). The emphasis on measuring investments in formal training, either in school or in the workplace, ignores the fact that individuals learn and acquire knowledge and skills in all kinds of social settings. A promising line of work is the design of learning environments based on constructivist views of learning and understanding (e.g., Collins, Brown, and Newman, 1989; Collins, Greeno, and Resnick, 1994; Collins, in press).

All these lines of research will benefit from adopting a sociocultural conception of skills that is attentive to the contexts of job, community of practice, and the workplace. Findings and conclusions based on such a contextual conception of skill will be cast in terms that are appropriate for informing effective policies to promote the skills that are required for success in the new workplace.

# BIBLIOGRAPHY

Anderson, J. (1983). *The Architecture of Cognition.* Cambridge, MA: Harvard University Press.

Appelbaum, E., and R. Batt (1993). *High-Performance Work Systems: American Models of Workplace Transformation.* Washington, DC: Economic Policy Institute.

Applebee, A. N. (1974). *Tradition and Reform in the Teaching of English: A History.* Urbana, IL: National Council of Teachers of English.

Attewell, P. (1990). "What Is Skill?" *Work and Occupations* 17(4): 422–448.

Bailey, T. (ed.) (1995). *Learning to Work: Employer Involvement in School-to-Work Transition Programs.* Washington, DC: The Brookings Institution.

Bailey, T. (1993a). "Can Youth Apprenticeship Thrive in the United States?" *Educational Researcher* 22(3):4–10.

Bailey, T. (1993b). *Discretionary Effort and the Organization of Work: Employee Participation and Work Reform Since Hawthorne.* Technical paper, National Center on Education and Employment.

Bailey, T., and D. Merritt. "Making Sense of Industry-Based Skills Standards," unpublished manuscript, Teachers College, Columbia University.

Barley, S. (1995). *The New Crafts: The Rise of the Technical Labor Force and its Implication for the Organization of Work.* Philadelphia, PA: University of Pennsylvania, National Center on the Educational Quality of the Workforce.

Berryman, S., and T. Bailey (1992). *The Double Helix of Education and the Economy, Executive Summary.* New York: Teachers College, Columbia University, Institute on Education and the Economy.

Bikson, T. K., B. A. Gutek, and D. Mankin (1981). *Implementing Computerized Procedures in Office Settings: Influences and Outcomes,* R-3308-OTA. Santa Monica, CA: RAND.

Bikson, T. K., and S. A. Law (1994). *Global Preparedness and Human Resources: College and Corporate Perspectives,* MR-326-CPC. Santa Monica, CA: RAND.

Bikson, T. K., and J. D. Eveland (1991). "Integrating New Tools with Information Work: Technology Transfer as a Framework for Understanding Success," in National Academy of Sciences, *People and Technology in the Workplace.* Washington, DC: National Academy Press, pp. 229–252.

Billett, S. (1993). Authenticity and a Culture of Practice Within Modes of Skill Development, *Australian and New Zealand Journal of Vocational Education Research* 2(1):1–29.

Black, J. (1994). "Cognitive Task Analysis," unpublished manuscript, Teachers College, Columbia University.

Black, J., E. Dimaraki, D. VanEsselstyn, and R. Flanagan (1995). "Using a Knowledge Representations Approach to Cognitive Task Analysis," unpublished manuscript, Teachers College, Columbia University.

Brown, J., A. Collins, and P. Duguid (1989). "Situated Cognition and the Culture of Learning," *Educational Researcher,* January–February:32–42.

Cappelli, P. (1992). *Is the "Skills Gap" Really About Attitudes?* EQW Working Paper. Philadelphia, PA: National Center on the Educational Quality of the Workforce.

Cappelli, P., and M. Ianozzi (1995). *Rethinking the Skills Gap: Is It Craft or Character?* Philadelphia, PA: University of Pennsylvania, National Center on the Educational Quality of the Workforce.

Cappelli, P., and N. Rogowsky (1995). *Skill Demands, Changing Work Organization, and Performance.* Philadelphia, PA: University of Pennsylvania, National Center on the Educational Quality of the Workforce.

Chi, M., R. Glaser, and M. Farr (eds.) (1988). *The Nature of Expertise.* Hillsdale, NJ: Lawrence Erlbaum Associates, Inc.

Cohen, E. (1994). Restructuring the Classroom: Conditions for Productive Small Groups, *Review of Educational Research* 64(1): 1–35.

Collins, A. (in press). "Design Issues for Learning Environments," to appear in S. Vosniadou, E. De Corte, R. Glaser, and H. Mandl (eds.), *International Perspectives on the Psychological Foundations of Technology-Based Learning Environments.* Hillsdale, NJ: Lawrence Erlbaum Associates, Inc.

Collins, A., J. Brown, and S. Newman (1989). "Cognitive Apprenticeship: Teaching the Craft of Reading, Writing, and Mathematics," in L. Resnick (ed.), *Knowing, Learning, and Instruction: Essays in Honor of Robert Glaser.* Hillsdale, NJ: Lawrence Erlbaum Associates, Inc.

Collins, A., J. Greeno, and L. Resnick (1994). "Learning Environments," in J. Husen and T. Postlewaite (eds.), *International Encyclopedia of Education* (2nd ed.). Oxford, UK: Pergamon.

Commission on the Skills of the American Workforce (1990). *America's Choice: High Skills or Low Wages.* Rochester, NY: National Center on Education and the Economy.

Corno, L. (1993). "The Best Laid Plans: Modern Conceptions of Volition and Educational Research," *Educational Researcher* 22(2):14–22.

Darrah, C. (1992). "Workplace Skills in Context," *Human Organization* 51(3):264–273.

Darrah, C. (1994). "Skill Requirements at Work: Rhetoric Versus Reality," *Work and Occupations* 21(1):64–84.

Dweck, C., and E. Elliott (1983). "Achievement Motivation," in E. M. Hetherington (ed.), *Handbook of Child Psychology* 4:643–691. New York: Wiley.

Dweck, C., and E. Leggett (1988). "A Social-Cognitive Approach to Motivation and Personality," *Psychological Review* 95:256–273.

Finegold, D., and D. Soskice (1988). "The Failure of Training in Britain: Analysis and Prescription," *Oxford Review of Economic Policy* Autumn:21–51.

Finegold, D. (1991). "Institutional Incentives and Skill Creation: Preconditions for a High-Skill Equilibrium," in P. Ryan (ed.), *International Comparisons of Vocational Education and Training for Intermediate Skills.* London: Falmer Press.

Finegold, D. (1992). "The Low-Skill Equilibrium: An Institutional Analysis of Britain's Education and Training Failure," submitted for degree, Pembroke College, Oxford, UK.

Geertz, C. (1973). *The Interpretation of Cultures.* New York: Basic Books.

Glaser, R., A. Lesgold, and S. Gott (1991). "Implications of Cognitive Psychology for Measuring Job Performance," in A. K. Wigdor and B. F Green (eds.), *Performance Assessment for the Workplace,* Vol. II, pp. 1–26. Washington, DC: National Academy Press.

Goetz, J., and M. LeCompte (1984). *Ethnography and Qualitative Design in Educational Research.* New York: Academic Press.

Grubb, W. N., T. Dickinson, L. Giordano, and G. Kaplan (1992). *Betwixt and Between: Education, Skills, and Employment in Sub-Baccalaureate Labor Markets.* Berkeley, CA: National Center for Research in Vocational Education.

Grubb, W. N., J. Kalman, M. Castellano, C. Brown, and D. Bradby (1991). *Readin', Writin', and 'Rithmetic One More Time: The Role of Remediation in Vocational Education and Job Training*

*Programs.*   Berkeley, CA:   National Center for Research in Vocational Education.

Grubb, W. N., and L. McDonnell (1991). *Local Systems of Vocational Education and Job Training: Diversity, Interdependence, and Effectiveness,* R-4077-NCRVE/UCB. Santa Monica, CA: RAND.

Hackman, J. R., and G. Oldham (1980). *Work Redesign.* Reading, MA: Addison-Wesley Publishing.

Hanser, L. M. (1995). *Traditional and Cognitive Job Analyses as Tools for Understanding the Skills Gap,* DRU-846-1-NCRVE/UCB. Santa Monica, CA: RAND.

Hart-Landsberg, S., J. Braunger, S. Reder, and M. Cross (1992). *Learning the Ropes: The Social Construction of Work-Based Learning,* MDS-413. Berkeley, CA: National Center for Research in Vocational Education.

Hudis, P., D. Bradby, C. Brown, E. G. Hoachlander, K. Levesque, and S. Nachuck (1992). *Meeting the Personnel Needs of the Health Care Industry Through Vocational Education Programs.* Berkeley, CA: National Center for Research in Vocational Education.

Hutchins, E. (1991). "The Social Organization of Distributed Cognition," in L. Resnick, J. Levine, and S. Teasley (eds.), *Perspectives on Socially Shared Cognition,* pp. 283–307. Washington, DC: American Psychological Association.

Kazis, R. (1993). *Improving the Transition from School to Work in the United States.* Washington, DC: American Youth Policy Forum.

Kinneavy, James L., *A Theory of Discourse: The Aims of Discourse,* New York: W. W. Norton, 1971, p. 18 ff.

Lave, J., and E. Wenger (1991). *Situated Learning: Legitimate Peripheral Participation.* Cambridge, MA: Cambridge University Press.

Lave, J. (1988). *Cognition in Practice: Mind, Mathematics, and Culture in Everyday Life.* Cambridge, MA: Cambridge University Press.

Lave, J. (1991). "Situating Learning in Communities of Practice," in L. Resnick, J. Levine, and S. Teasley (eds.), *Perspectives on Socially Shared Cognition*, pp. 63–82. Washington, DC: American Psychological Association.

Levine, A., and J. Luck (1994). *The New Management Paradigm: A Review of Principles and Practices*, MR-458-AF. Santa Monica, CA: RAND.

Levine, J., and R. Moreland (1991). "Culture and Socialization in Work Groups," in L. Resnick, J. Levine, and S. Teasley (eds.), *Perspectives on Socially Shared Cognition*, pp. 257–279. Washington, DC: American Psychological Association.

Lillard, L., and H. Tan (1986). *Private Sector Training: Who Gets It and What Are Its Effects?* R-3331-DOL/RC. Santa Monica, CA: RAND.

Lincoln, Y., and E. Guba (1985). *Naturalistic Inquiry.* Beverly Hills, CA: Sage Publications.

Marshall, R., and M. Tucker (1992). *Thinking for a Living: Education and the Wealth of Nations.* New York: Basic Books.

Martin, L., and K. Beach (1992). *Technical and Symbolic Knowledge in CNC Machining: A Study of Technical Workers of Different Backgrounds.* Berkeley, CA: National Center for Research in Vocational Education.

McGraw, K. and R. Forrant (1992). *A Worker's Perspective: Skills, Training, and Education in the Automotive Repair, Printing, and Metalworking Trades.* Berkeley, CA: National Center for Research in Vocational Education.

National Assessment of Vocational Education (NAVE) (1994). *Final Report to Congress*, Volume I: *Summary and Recommendations.* Washington, DC: U.S. Department of Education, Office of Educational Research and Improvement.

National Center on the Educational Quality of the Workforce (NCEQW) (1995). *EQW National Employer Survey (EQW-NES).* Philadelphia, PA: University of Pennsylvania.

Natriello, G. (1989). *What do Employers Want in Entry-Level Workers? An Assessment of the Evidence,* NCEE Occasional Paper No. 7. New York: Teachers College, Columbia University.

Newell, A., and H. Simon (1972). *Human Problem Solving.* Englewood Cliffs, NJ: Prentice-Hall.

Orr, J. (1991). *Talking About Machines: An Ethnography of a Modern Job.* PARC Technical Report SSL-91-07 (P9100132), Palo Alto, CA: Xerox PARC.

Patton, M. (1980). *Qualitative Evaluation Methods.* Beverly Hills, CA: Sage Publications.

Perkins, D., E. Jay, and S. Tishman (1993a). "New Conceptions of Thinking: From Ontology to Education," *Educational Psychologist* 28(1):67–85.

Perkins, D., E. Jay, and S. Tishman (1993b). "Beyond Abilities: A Dispositional Theory of Thinking," *Merrill-Palmer Quarterly* 39(1):1–21.

Perkins, D., and G. Salomon (1989). "Are Cognitive Skills Context-Bound?" *Educational Researcher* January–February:16–25.

Prawat, R. S. (1989). "Promoting Access to Knowledge, Strategy, and Dispositions in Students: A Research Synthesis," *Review of Educational Research* 59(1):1–41.

Raizen, S. (1989). *Reforming Education for Work: A Cognitive Science Perspective.* Berkeley, CA: University of California, Berkeley, National Center for Research in Vocational Education.

Ray, C. A., and R. A. Mickelson (1993). "Restructuring Students for Restructured Work: The Economy, School Reform, and Non-college-bound Youths," *Sociology of Education* 66:1–20.

Reich, R. (1991). *The Work of Nations: Preparing Ourselves for 21st-Century Capitalism.* New York: Vintage Books.

Resnick, L. (1991). "Shared Cognition: Thinking As Social Practice," in L. Resnick, J. Levine, and S. Teasley (eds.), *Perspectives on Socially Shared Cognition,* pp. 1–20. Washington, DC: American Psychological Association.

Rogers, J., and W. Streeck (1991). *Skill Needs and Training Strategies in the Wisconsin Metalworking Industry.* Madison, WI: University of Wisconsin-Madison.

Rogoff, B., and P. Charajay (1995). "What's Become of Research on the Cultural Basis of Cognitive Development?" *American Psychologist* 50(10):859–877.

Schultz, K. (1992). *Training for Basic Skills or Educating Workers?: Changing Conceptions of Workplace Education Programs.* Berkeley, CA: National Center for Research in Vocational Education.

Scribner, S., and P. Sachs (1990). *A Study of On-the-Job Training,* Technical Paper No. 13. New York: Institute on Education and the Economy, Teachers College, Columbia University.

Scribner, S. (1988). *Head and Hand: An Action Approach to Thinking,* Occasional Paper No. 3. New York: National Center on Education and Employment.

Scribner, S., P. Sachs, L. DiBello, and J. Kindred (1993). *Knowledge Acquisition at Work.* New York: IEE Publications.

Scribner, S. (1984). "Studying Working Intelligence," in B. Rogoff and J. Lave (eds.), *Everyday Cognition: Its Development in Social Context.* Cambridge, MA: Harvard University Press.

Secretary's Commission on Achieving Necessary Skills (SCANS) (1991). *What Work Requires of Schools.* Washington, DC: U.S. Department of Labor.

Secretary's Commission on Achieving Necessary Skills (SCANS) (1992a). *Learning a Living: A Blueprint for High Performance.* Washington, DC: U.S. Department of Labor.

Secretary's Commission on Achieving Necessary Skills (SCANS) (1992b). *Skills and Tasks for Jobs.* Washington, DC: U.S. Department of Labor.

Soskice, D. (1991). "Skill Mismatch, Training Systems and Equilibrium Unemployment: A Comparative Institutional

Analysis," in F. Padoa-Schioppa (ed.), *Mismatch and Labor Mobility*. Cambridge, MA: CNP.

Spenner, K. (1990). "Skill: Meanings, Methods, and Measures," *Work and Occupations* 17(4):399–421.

Spradley, J. P. (1980). *Participant Observation*. New York: Holt, Rinehart, and Winston.

Stasz, C. (1995). *The Economic Imperative Behind School Reform: A Review of the Literature*, DRU-1064-NCRVE/UCB. Santa Monica, CA: RAND.

Stasz, C., D. McArthur, M. Lewis, and K. Ramsey (1990). *Teaching and Learning Generic Skills for the Workplace*, R-4004-NCRVE/UCB. Santa Monica, CA: RAND.

Stasz, C., K. Ramsey, R. Eden, J. DaVanzo, H. Farris, and M. Lewis (1993). *Classrooms That Work: Teaching Generic Skills in Academic and Vocational Settings*, MR-169-NCRVE/UCB. Santa Monica, CA: RAND.

Stasz, C., T. Kaganoff, and R. Eden (1994). "Integrating Academic and Vocational Education: A Review of the Literature, 1987–1992," *Journal of Vocational Education Research* 19(2):25–77.

Stern, D. (1994). *Human Resource Development in a Learning-Based Economy*, paper prepared for OECD conference "Employment and Growth in the Knowledge-Based Economy," Copenhagen, November 7–8, 1994.

Teixeira, R., and L. Mishel (Summer, 1993). "Whose Skills Shortage—Workers or Management?" *Issues in Science and Technology*.

U.S. Congress, Office of Technology Assessment (OTA) (1990). *Worker Training: Competing in the New International Economy*, OTA-ITE-457. Washington, DC: U.S. Government Printing Office.

Vaughn, R., and S. Berryman (1989). *Employer-Sponsored Training: Current Status, Future Possibilities*. New York: Teachers College, Columbia University.

Veum, J. (August, 1993). "Training Among Young Adults: Who, What Kind, and For How Long?" *Monthly Labor Review*.

Vygotsky, L. (1978). *Mind in Society: The Development of Higher Psychological Processes*. Cambridge, MA: Harvard University Press.

Yin, R. K. (1981). "The Case Study as a Serious Research Strategy," *Knowledge, Creation, Diffusion, Utilization*, 3:97–114.

Yin, R. K. (1994). *Case Study Research: Design and Methods*, Second Edition. Thousand Oaks, CA: Sage Publications.